THE

RULES

OF

REVISION

...

10 successful students help
you achieve outstanding
exam results

ISBN-13: 978-0-9930429-7-3

Disclaimer

The authors of this publication give no guarantee of improved examination performance nor will they be held responsible for any mistakes that may appear in this publication. They are not responsible if this publication, in any way, has a detrimental effect on its reader(s) or any other persons. This publication offers suggestions that have produced results for the authors, but does not in any way state that these methods are the only ways of succeeding in examinations.

Table of Contents

INTRODUCTION

Who are we?

Liam Porritt
(University of Cambridge, Modern Languages)

Joe Tyler
(University of Cambridge, Land Economy)

Nat Trueman
(University of Cambridge, Engineering)

Alex van Leeuwen
(University of Oxford, Classics)

Becky Brooks
(University of Cambridge, Linguistics)

David Morris
(University of Cambridge, Engineering)

Kat Savvas
(University of Cambridge, Modern Languages)

Alexia Michaelidou
(University of Cambridge, Law)

Cameron Anderson
(University of Cambridge, Philosophy)

Adam Bennett
(University of Cambridge, Modern Languages)

Why should you read this?

Starting this book with a list of the ten people who've contributed to it may seem a little pretentious, particularly given that 'University of Cambridge' or 'University of Oxford' appears next to every single one of their names.

Perhaps it is a little pretentious. But it's there for two reasons:

1. To ensure you understand that the advice offered in this book comes straight from people who've already achieved exactly what you're after: academic success.
2. To motivate you to want to read this book and get everything you possibly can out of it so that you go away and succeed like the ten of us.

Between us, we've read a selection of the best-selling study guides available. We've researched exactly how the most successful students get the results they are after. And, most importantly of all, we've sat in your shoes, seeking exam success, and we've discovered exactly how to deliver it.

CAN THIS BOOK HELP YOU?

There are three types of person who may be reading this book:

1. Those who are driven towards success, want to know how to succeed and are prepared to work hard and implement the rules that will be laid out here.
2. Those who are looking to succeed and believe that just reading this will enable them to do so, magically transforming them into machines who know all the answers to every possible exam question.
3. Those who don't care about success, have been forced into reading this book by their parents and are not driven to improve their future with hard work.

WHICH ARE YOU?

If you are the third, it is key that you understand that – no matter how rigorously you read this book – no one else – no matter how much time, effort and money they pump into trying to make you succeed – is able to *make* you succeed. We live in a world that is more competitive than ever before and if you want to achieve, and I firmly believe that anyone can, it has to come from you, not your hopeful parents or desperate teachers. So, if you cannot come to terms with that, go away until you are comfortable in the knowledge that it is only with your own commitment and hard work that you *will* succeed – and trust me, you will.

> *Genius is 1% inspiration and 99% perspiration. Accordingly a genius is often merely a talented person who has done all of his or her homework.*
>
> Thomas Edison

STILL HERE?

... Or just got back, having considered what I said before? Good. That means you are now in either the first or second category. You are already on the road towards exam success, taking the first step by realising that it is *you*, and no one but you, who must want to succeed in order to do so.

However, although this book seeks to minimise the amount of time you need to spend revising by maximising your efficiency during the revision process, it is not a magic potion – even if it comes pretty close! As obvious as this may sound, just by reading this, you won't suddenly be able to answer every question the examiners could throw at you. If you are currently in the second category, you must reposition yourself up into the first one, understanding that hard work, along with the right techniques provided by the rules set out in this guide, will be necessary for you to make the most of your potential.

WHAT WILL THIS BOOK DO?

This book is specifically designed to ensure that you maximise your potential by using the tried and tested methods of students at some of the best universities in the world:

- In the run up to revision
- While revising
- During the exams themselves

THE BUSINESSMAN OR WOMAN

Think of yourself as a businessman or woman. Instead of earning money, you are earning marks. The rich find ways of making money and stick to those methods; this book will allow you to do exactly the same, providing straightforward methods to help you earn marks when you get into the exam-room.

The simple fact is that the majority of students want to obtain the best possible grades, it's just that some know how to revise and sit exams to ensure they maximise their potential, where others have no idea. What and how you revise have a huge impact on your end performance: just because you spent hours every day sat at a desk in the run-up to your exams does not necessarily mean that you will get a good grade.

Again, I use the analogy of a businessman or woman: if I sell clothing made by up-and-coming brands and I set up a stall at a car-boot sale where the majority of customers are over 50, I could spend a whole day there and sell very little. If, by contrast, I set up at a high-end music festival, full of young people with money to spend, I could spend an hour at this venue and sell more than I did in a day at the car-boot sale. Ultimately, revision is the same: it is not purely a case of how much time you spend revising; how, where and when you revise are also crucial.

Executing the plan

So, this book will help you make the most of the time you spend revising. However, this still leaves a potential problem: there's nothing more agonising than spending hours revising for an exam and then making stupid mistakes under exam pressure that ruin your mark. We aim to show you how to prevent doing just that by improving your exam technique, enabling you, when it matters most, to execute the plan: obtain the highest marks possible.

Rock or sand? Mansion or shack?

A wise man built his house on a rock. The man laid a strong foundation by digging deep into the earth. A stupid or foolish man built his house on the sand. This man did not build a strong, deep foundation and built his house very quickly.

The parable of the Two Builders: Matthew 7:24-27, Luke 6:47-49

The foundation you lay is equivalent to your revision.

You can either lay a solid foundation on which to build a sturdy exam performance or you can build a weak and rushed foundation that leaves you little hope of exam success. Once you've laid your foundation (done your revision), your exam technique will build you a house: good exam technique builds a mansion while poor exam technique builds a shack.

How to use this book

Prioritise

Just as with your revision, you should feel free to read the parts that most apply to you. Look at the title of each rule and see whether you think you'll find that useful. If not, move on.

That said, many of the rules go into more detail on some of the basic principles of revision, offering you specific advice on how to implement stuff you already know, such as that you should 'plan your revision' or 'revise actively'.

Skip around

For you, not all rules will have been created equal! If you find you are reading something that isn't useful, just skip onto the next section or rule.

Implement what you read

Perhaps most importantly of all, it is crucial that you don't just think: 'ooohh, that's a good idea', and then forget all about it as soon as you close this book.

You need to make a conscious effort during your study or revision sessions, while practicing for exams and during the exams themselves to implement any rules you think will help you succeed.

Plan to Succeed

WHAT'S THIS SECTION ABOUT?

Given that you're reading this book, you've already demonstrated to yourself that you want to revise more effectively and, ultimately, obtain the best grades possible. Therefore, I have no doubt that you intend to spend time over the coming weeks, months or maybe even years working and revising in preparation for your exams. However, it is crucial that you spend this time wisely, planning your days so that you make the most of each revision slot and ensuring that you don't drift aimlessly through notes, textbooks and past papers.

Therefore, you need a revision plan! This is obvious and is probably the first thing anyone with the vaguest idea about revision would tell you. In fact, I suspect the vast majority of the people reading this always plan their revision anyway. However, the following rules will ensure that both your preparation before beginning revision and your revision plan maximise your efficiency and concentration once you begin revising. There is far more to planning and organising than the following:

11:00am – 1:00pm	English
1:30pm – 2:30pm	LUNCH!!
2:30pm – 4:30pm	Maths

A plan is also hugely important in keeping you motivated for revision. It will mean you have a fixed amount of time during which to achieve your revision goals – somewhat preferable to aimlessly drifting through your notes for hours and achieving very little!

LEARN IT IN THE FIRST PLACE (BY JOE TYLER)

The introduction to this section on planning for success mentioned that it would cover preparation before beginning revision, as well as the planning phase. What is this 'preparation before beginning revision'? It is perhaps the best way that you can maximise your revision efficiency: learn stuff in the first place!

WHY A LOT OF PEOPLE STRUGGLE

I think a lot of people approach revision in the wrong way.

They believe it consists solely of reviewing notes in the run-up to exams or reading a dull and dry textbook late into the night in the hope that their mind will somehow absorb information. The reality, however, is that effective revision is a lengthy process that lasts from the moment you start a course until the day you sit your exams.

The initial, and in my opinion most important, part of the revision process is effective learning of information when it is first seen. Hearing a piece of information in a classroom does not equate to learning it and, equally, reading from a textbook does not mean you've understood, or will remember, what you've read. In fact, even completing a number of practice questions set by your teacher and achieving a good mark does not mean that you understand the topic. Many people will have simply regurgitated information from a textbook or website.

REVIEW LITTLE AND OFTEN

It is essential that you spend time, after covering something in a lesson, reviewing it and ensuring that you understand it. How can you do this? Allocate 15-30 minutes of your evening, and then perhaps 1 hour at the end of the week to quickly go over the work you've done that day or week for each subject, asking yourself:

> "Do I understand what we covered in this topic?"

If the answer is yes, brilliant. If it is no, then spend a few minutes trying to get to grips with it. If you still can't get your head around it, annotate the tricky part or mark it with a sticky note and ask your teacher to explain it to you.

Trust me, spending this time to quickly review what you've covered will save you far more time when it comes to revising. If you don't trust me, trust the science: here is something called the Ebbinghaus Curve of Forgetting.

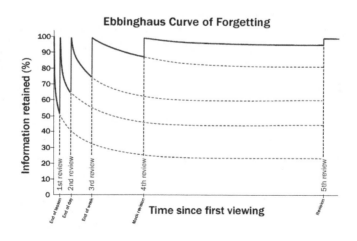

Ebbinghaus Curve of Forgetting

This graph shows that, if you fail to review the material you cover in class at the end of the day and week, you'll have to begin your revision with around 20% retention, as opposed to 40%-70% retention with these two reviews. Not reviewing your class notes, as opposed to reviewing them at the end of the day and week, translates to about twice as much time spent revising!

> **66% of material is forgotten within 7 days if it is not revisited.**

You'll have noticed on the graph that I included suggestions of when you might perform each of the 5 reviews it shows. Admittedly, you're pretty unlikely to complete *all* of these reviews. That said, if you can complete just 3 or 4 of them, you'll be in a pretty strong position when you come to take your exams. You may also have seen that the first review can happen at the end of your lesson! So, while everyone else is scrambling their stuff together to leave as quickly as possible, spend 30-60 seconds glancing over the class notes you've just made. This counts as your first review, so why not make the most of this time?

Do your homework

Loads of students seem to see homework as pointless. Or at least they struggle to see why they should have to spend so long on it. However, when we consider the importance of reviewing what you study to increase the amount of information retained, it becomes clear that homework is actually an extremely useful way of completing one of these reviews.

In fact, because homework really tests your understanding of the material you've covered, it is even better than just reviewing what you covered in class. It forces you to go through your class notes, searching for the information needed to answer the questions. It then also makes you manipulate that information so that you can answer the specific question being asked.

Finally, you then get the privilege of seeing exactly how well your reviewing session went when your teachers returns your homework back to you.

> *Look for where you went wrong and learn from your mistakes.*

Study for mock exams

Similarly to above, you shouldn't see mock exams as 'a waste of your time', you should see them as a brilliant opportunity to review what you've been learning and then test out how well your studying has been going: mock exams are a brilliant indicator (when you work for them) of how effective your studying has been and of how much harder you need to work before the real things.

Discuss with a study buddy or teacher

From my personal experience, I believe that the best way to attain a genuine understanding of a topic is to discuss it, both with other students and, if possible, with teachers. Discussing topics is a great way of reviewing them and can also really help to improve your understanding.

If you struggle with a question on your homework, why not discuss it with your study buddy? If you fail to understand something when you review your class notes, why not ask your teacher about it at the start of your next lesson? Never be afraid to discuss and ask questions.

REVIEWING WILL PAY OFF LATER

In the final run-up to your exams (I know that's a long way off at the moment – this is only the first rule!) the priority must be to do past papers. Reviewing your notes in order to increase the amount of information retained will give you more time later on to complete past papers without having to waste precious time trawling through textbooks and notes attempting to revise topics that you may barely remember learning in the first place.

If you spend a little extra time during the year learning the information properly rather than just revising in the run-up to your exams you'll save a whole lot of time and stress in the later stages.

Effective first learning of information can be thought of as a way of working smarter rather than necessarily harder, giving yourself loads more time to work on your exam technique in the latter stages of your revision.

SORT OUT YOUR FILING SYSTEM

If you haven't already done so, get your subject folders and notes organised immediately. Invest in some ring binders and dividers (and plastic wallets if you want, although these make it more inconvenient to annotate notes while revising). Make sure you do the following:

- Have a separate folder for each subject
- Ensure this folder only contains material related to topics on the syllabus (get rid of anything which cannot appear on the exam paper)
- Split this folder up into different topics using file dividers

These folders can then be used as easy reference points when you want to make condensed revision notes or when you come across something in a past paper you don't understand. They will also make you feel a lot more positive about your revision, as you can systematically go through each folder, revising each topic, with the obvious added benefit that you are far less likely to miss out a topic, or forget to revise something if your file is well organised into topic areas.

When beginning my revision, I normally spend the first day drawing up a revision plan and sifting through all of my files, sorting any loose paper into a topic section and ensuring that everything is in order. This day is well worth the effort as it will save you hours in the long-run, meaning you are actually revising, rather than searching for a piece of paper amongst thousands of sheets in tens of folders.

PLAN YOURSELF

There is a broad array of very popular, online tools you can use to plan your revision. However, of all of the successful students I've spoken to, it seems very few of us use these online planning tools.

WHY SHOULDN'T YOU USE THEM?

The simple reason is that life is far more complicated and unexpected than a machine could ever understand. Online revision planners may, for example, give you the ability to input certain hobbies that happen on a weekly basis. However, they can't possibly anticipate that your friend, who you had planned to meet on Wednesday afternoon, may remember that he has a dentist's appointment then, so you need to rearrange to meet on Thursday instead.

Admittedly, you can't anticipate that either, but planning yourself on a piece of paper gives you far greater control over when you are revising what. It gives you the ability to scribble over your original agenda without feeling like you are destroying your perfectly printed plan produced online.

FEEL IN CONTROL

Even more importantly, if you're finding a particular subject more difficult than anticipated, you're unlikely to change and then reprint your online plan, sticking to the original schedule, even if it isn't quite right for you. However, when you plan yourself, you are in full control of your own revision. This increased responsibility, as you choose to revise for a certain amount of time each day – because you want to, not because your computer is telling you to – gives you a greater sense of pride and motivation.

Plan Realistically

Plan to do as much revision as you know you can! If you can concentrate on revision for about 5 hours a day (and after that you won't learn anything) plan to do 5 hours a day... No more, no less! Having said this, the number of hours you can possibly do needs to be the upper limit of your concentration capacity. You need to ask yourself:

> "If I really put my mind to it, how long can I spend concentrating on revision?"

My advice would be that it should be somewhere between 4 and 6 hours a day.

> *Don't give yourself an unrealistic amount of work to do each day.*

There is no point planning to do more than you are capable of as this will lead to frustration over the fact that you are not achieving as much as you would like and, more importantly, will mean that some of the material you need to revise does not get covered before your exams start because you've not been able to keep up with your revision schedule.

PLAN PRECISELY

Revising without a plan is like finding somewhere without a map: you don't know where you're going or how long the journey will take.

Robert Blakey (author of *I Hate Revision*)

Your revision timetable will be most useful if you plan specific time slots during which you'll either be revising or having a break. This means that you know exactly when each session starts and ends and how long you've been working for. The advantage of this is three-fold:

1. If you start and end at specific times, there is no risk of you cutting short your revision time, for example saying that you'll work for 45 minutes and actually only doing 38.
2. You have a target to aim for. If you work hard during a time slot, you'll be able to stop and have a rewarding break when that slot finishes. This means that you'll be far more motivated to work than if you just start work at some point and go on for as long as you can until you get bored, which probably won't take very long!
3. If you repeat the time slots every day, your body clock will begin to adjust itself to these working hours with routine taking over, meaning that it is actually easier for your body to conform to this revision routine than to break out of this 'natural' cycle.

Rule 5: Plan Precisely

As well as planning precise times, make sure you plan exact topics to be revising. I normally only plan the topics I need to cover for the next three days as it's impossible to know exactly how long each of these will take and exactly how productive I'm going to be during each revision slot. However, it is important to plan which specific areas you'll cover (bearing in mind all of the topics and making sure you don't spend too long on one to the detriment of another).

GIVE YOURSELF SMALL GOALS & REWARDS

It is human nature to enjoy instantaneous satisfaction rather than the promise of future rewards.

> *Do you want £10 now or in a year's time? Obvious: NOW!*

Of course, if I asked you do you want £10 now or £1000 in a year's time, you would probably be willing to wait in order to gain more money later on. However, the issue comes when you cannot quantify or directly compare the short-term satisfaction against the future benefits of long-term revision. The promise of future rewards gained by revising hard far outweighs the small amount of instant satisfaction gained from watching TV, but because the two cannot be directly compared and there is no way of quantifying how much more you'll gain from revising rather than relaxing, you find it incredibly tempting to derive immediate satisfaction from watching TV!

Clearly there is one other major difference between my analogy of offering you £10 now or £1000 in a year's time and the real choice you face between sitting in front of a TV or at a desk: effort! Whereas to gain an extra £990 you simply have to wait an extra year (something that requires no actual effort on your part), in order to revise instead of watching TV you have to put in effort that could be saved by watching TV.

Therefore, while you should also keep the promise of long-term rewards in your mind when revising, you also need to find a way to both give yourself instantaneous gratification from revision and motivate yourself to put in the extra effort required by revision over watching TV.

There are two components that, together, can combat these basic human desires for both instant satisfaction and minimal exertion:

1. Set yourself challenging goals so that when you achieve them, you gain a sense of immediate satisfaction. This means that you must plan to complete a certain amount of revision in the time allocated to a specific revision slot. So, rather than writing '1 hour – Biology' in your plan, decide before you begin the slot what you want to achieve and write '1 hour – Biology, make condensed revision notes on reproduction (All)'. This way, when you get to the end of each revision slot and the end of each day, you'll feel that you've actually achieved a goal rather than having simply spent another hour blankly starring at a biology textbook. This technique also makes spending effort far more worthwhile because you can actually quantify the amount of progress made from the effort you are putting in rather than putting in effort and seemingly gaining nothing.
2. Reward yourself with things you like (could be material things or time spent doing things you enjoy) when you complete your goals. You must be disciplined with yourself or get someone else (such as your parents) to make sure you are disciplined and only allow these rewards once you've completed your goals. By turning revision into something you have to do in order to see your

friends, for example, you not only gain the satisfaction of accomplishing your revision goals but also give yourself short-term fulfilment between revision slots. In this way, you can transform your instinctive desire to use as little effort as possible into a positive force that makes you want to work harder during your revision slots so that you can then enjoy the following reward.

DON'T LOSE SIGHT OF THE BIGGER PICTURE

While detailed planning and small goals are essential to maximising your revision efficiency, it is definitely a good idea to have a broad plan of what you need to cover week-by-week so that you can track your overall progress, systematically working towards your ultimate end goal: exam success. As you achieve your weekly revision goals, you'll be safe in the knowledge that you are on course to finish revising all of the content before each of your exams, preventing a scenario I know all too well from when I sat mock exams aged 15.

THE 'TUNNEL VISION' SCENARIO

Having drawn up detailed plans of what I would be covering day-by-day for three day periods several times over the course of two and a half weeks, I was suddenly struck by the panicked realisation that I was miles behind where I should have been, with just a week until my exams got underway.

Having set out no long-term plan, I had gradually fallen behind in the two or three subjects I found most difficult. I had stuck precisely to my allocated timeslots for each subject but, within some of these slots, I simply hadn't been getting through the different topics as quickly as I needed to. I was suddenly plunged into a shocked state of realisation, struck by three distinct reasons for my severe under-preparation.

The Brutal Realisation That...

1. I had been trying to cover everything in greater detail than I really needed. I had been testing myself on things I already knew and had been wasting time with excessively detailed notes that actually did very little to help me.

2. During my revision slots, Facebook had been a force of total evil, giving me a welcome, but unnecessary distraction every time my phone flashed up with a notification. I knew I shouldn't have been spending so much time on it, but did nothing to try and stop myself from aimlessly scrolling down my Newsfeed while I should have been working.

3. Up until that point, I naively hadn't realised that I wasn't going to get through all of the topics before my exam if I continued at the rate I was going. Having begun to slip behind, I had been blissfully unaware that I was spending time covering topics I should have already finished. I failed to see that I needed to either speed up in or spend more time on the subjects I found most difficult so that I would finish my revision in time for the mock exams.

So, a week from my exams, I was really shaken up by just how underprepared I was in a few of my subjects.

The first two realisations above will be dealt with later on in this guide when we get on to the actual process of revising. (Look at pg. 63 for help with different styles of revision and pg. 107 to help you avoid distractions.)

However, it was the third that was probably the most painful of all and the one that I have, ever since, been extremely keen to avoid – I still remember that sinking, sickening feeling in the pit of my stomach as it dawned on me just how little I had covered.

Start with a broad plan

Having a precise plan is crucial. However, before you start going into lots of detail, planning every second of your life for a few days at a time, you should plan broadly. This means:

- Putting together a list of the overarching topics for each of the subjects you study.
- Working out how many of these topics need to be covered per week to finish ahead of your exams.
- Planning, week-by-week, the topics you'll complete for each subject so that you finish on time. Bear in mind that you should leave yourself enough time to go over any areas you've struggled with. You should also plan to leave time for practicing a few past papers under exam conditions, having completed your revision of each of the examination topics. I would recommend completing your revision of all of the topics for a subject at least one week ahead of the exam for that subject.

Remove the blinkers when planning precisely

I advise that you review how your revision is progressing roughly twice a week when making your precise plan, ensuring you don't fall behind your broader schedule.

BE FLEXIBLE & HAVE CONTINGENCY SLOTS

Previous rules have told you to plan your revision realistically and precisely, while also keeping an eye on the bigger picture.

In an ideal world, once you had made a plan you would stick to it exactly. This never happens because the world is not ideal and things always come up that mean you may miss a slot or even most of a day. Equally, you could have a day when you are feeling ill or just not in the frame of mind for revision (although with the techniques in this book, that shouldn't happen). Therefore, it is crucial that your plan is flexible.

As such, while you should break each day down into precise and manageable chunks, you should also be prepared to be flexible with those chunks, building contingency slots into your plan for when you fall behind schedule.

Life belongs to the living, and he who lives must be prepared for changes.

Johann Wolfgang von Goethe (German writer, statesman & philosopher)

By ensuring you build in these contingency slots, you give yourself a safety net if you don't finish a topic when you were expecting to, preventing you from falling behind your broader revision plan.

REVISE EARLY (BY NAT TRUEMAN)

When planning your revision, 'revising early' has two equally important meanings.

DON'T BE LAST-MINUTE

Firstly, it is crucial that you don't leave all of your revision to the last minute, beginning your revision as long before your exams as is reasonably possible. This is obvious, but resisting the temptation to put-off revision because your "exams aren't for ages" is paramount if you want to ensure you cover all of the material for all of your subjects.

Get cracking as early as possible and you'll have 3 months of summer to enjoy in the knowledge that you did the best you could have done in your exams. If you don't work now you'll have two problems:

1. You won't be able to retain all of the information you need by 'cramming' or 'pulling all-nighters'.
2. You'll panic! You will, the week or the night before the exam, know that you have not done enough work.

You'll sleep badly, be less focused, be less calm, be more likely to make stupid mistakes and most of all will lack confidence in your own ability to succeed!

GET UP AND GO

Secondly, it is vital that you realise that revision is most productive earlier on in the day. As much as you may love staying up late and getting up late, this lifestyle won't come close to the 'early-bird' way of life in terms of revision productivity.

Getting up early, having a good breakfast and then beginning revision somewhere between 9:00 and 10:00 (we aren't talking ridiculously early here!) will mean that you get far more done during the hours when your brain is most receptive to information. During the time before lunch, you should aim to get around 50% of your work for the day completed.

Then, after lunch, it is wise to plan:

- Shorter time slots for learning-based revision
- To do a different, more active form of revision such as a past paper or questions from a revision guide (see the next rule for more on this).

As both of these will ensure that your mind stays more focussed following a morning of hard, intense work.

> *Morning is wonderful. Its only drawback is that it comes at such an inconvenient time of day.*
>
> Glen Cook (author of *Sweet Silver Blues*)

PLAN DIFFERENT TYPES OF REVISION

Regardless of how motivated you are, everyone gets bored and distracted during revision. The key to success is in maximising the amount of time you can spend revising before you get bored while minimising your chances of becoming distracted during your revision. We'll deal with the latter issue later in the book when we come onto the actual process of revising (pg. 107).

As for maximising the amount of time you can spend revising, it is simply not the case that some people are naturally able to plough on revising for hours where others struggle to reach ten minutes. What is really happening is that those who seem to be able to concentrate for longer have planned to revise in different ways throughout the day, while those who struggle to get to ten minutes have barely planned their revision at all.

REVISE 'ACTIVELY' – WHAT DOES THIS EVEN MEAN?

When it comes to the revision process itself, my advice would be that you use whichever revision methods suit you – you'll come across quite a few in Rule 22 starting on pg. 63. However, when it comes to planning, the most important thing is that you plan to revise 'actively'.

This is an expression that people in the education sector throw around a lot, but it's not always entirely clear what it actually means! It simply means that you must be doing things to make you learn the information rather than just reading text and expecting yourself to remember it. As you'll discover in more depth later (pg. 67), I personally prefer to write brief but key notes on a topic, condensing the information from class notes and textbooks into titled lists of information. Alternatively, I use a revision guide that already contains all of the information condensed down – Exam Grade Booster aims to produce exactly this type of resource. Once I have this condensed information, I'll then probably have a read through it on another day, highlighting key words or parts I don't know very well as I go, trying to memorise the information. Finally, I go through testing

> **Note**
> You can see here from this outline of my own revision method that I am revising 'actively' – I am always doing things to help my brain retain the information rather than merely reading through class notes or textbooks.

myself on each piece of information, marking and going over what I get wrong, and repeating the process until I think I know it all.

WHAT SHOULD YOUR PLAN INCLUDE?

So, if we take the example of how I like to revise, the building blocks (the most basic 'types') of revision are:

1. Making condensed revision notes, mind maps, quote lists etc.
2. Revising from guides, notes, mind maps etc. by reading, highlighting, reproducing and further condensing
3. Learning material by testing yourself or getting others to test you

Add to these types of revision doing questions from revision guides or wherever else and doing past papers and you have five different types of revision that you should be planning to use each day.

When to do what

The previous rule advised you to revise early. On top of starting early, I believe there are some types of revision that are better done in the morning, while others can be left for later in the day when you are a little more tired.

I would recommend that your first 'type' of revision each day is note-making, in whatever format you choose to use (lists, mind-maps etc.), as it is best to do this while your mind is at its freshest. Reading, highlighting, reproducing and further condensing these notes is also most effective if it is done in the morning.

As the day progresses, I would recommend you begin to include some of the more innovative techniques (there are plenty of them in Rule 22), such as *Kat's Paper Prompter*, in order to prevent distraction as much as possible and keep your mind engaged. You should also switch to the most active forms of revision at some point in the afternoon, either doing past papers or questions from a revision guide, as you'll find these types of revision are best at preventing distraction.

> *During a day, I would try to fit in as many different types of revision as possible.*

In the morning, I would make a form of revision material (condensed notes in my case) and I would test myself on some other notes I had already made for another subject. I would then repeat this up until lunch. Then, in the afternoon, I would do a past paper for a decent length of time and another, slightly different form of revision such as a French listening test, recording myself speaking Spanish oral answers or a bit of online, interactive learning.

This combination of revision types, planned so that the most arduous forms happen in the morning, will ensure that you minimise boredom during revision and that your brain retains the maximum amount of information. These ideas on when to do what are not hard and fast rules, but they should help you to remain focused on your revision for the maximum length of time possible.

Take Breaks... But, How Often ? How Long ?

This is one of the most hotly contested issues in education: how long can you concentrate for before you need a break and how long should you then take a break for? However, the truth is you need to work out (pretty quickly) what works for you. As stated in Rule 9, I would recommend making revision slots longer in the morning and shorter in the evening, and would also recommend longer afternoon breaks. What is more, how long you can concentrate for depends on the type of revision you are doing. Therefore, when planning, I would allocate (depending on the time of day of the revision slot) the following amounts of time to each type of revision:

Type of Revision	Length of Slot
Making condensed revision notes, mind maps, quote lists etc.	AM: 40mins - 1hr PM: 40 - 50mins
Revising from guides, notes, mind maps etc. by reading, highlighting, reproducing & further condensing	AM: 35 - 50mins PM: 30 - 40mins
Learning material by testing myself or getting others to test me	AM: 30 - 45mins PM: 30 - 40mins
Answering questions from a revision guide, sheet or other source	AM: 40mins - 1hr PM: 40 - 50mins
Doing past papers	All day: 1 – 3hrs

> **Note**
> These 'types of revision' are very broad, but should give you an idea of how long you can concentrate for when using each general revision technique. For loads of much more specific revision techniques to use in the run-up to your exams, turn to pg. 63, *Know How You Revise*. You may even like to include some of these techniques in your plan, although you can also use them spontaneously throughout the revision process, within the allocated time slots.

In my opinion, that table is a pretty good guide for anyone (of any ability). The times given are not exact, and if I were storming through, making amazing revision notes for a subject, I wouldn't necessarily stop when my timetable told me to if I didn't feel like I needed a break (although this is pretty rare). As I've said previously (Rules 5 & 8), you should plan your revision precisely, but also be prepared to be flexible.

So, we've seen how often to break, but then the question is how long should you break for? This really is a matter of personal preference. From a little research I've done into students' revision performance, 43 out of 50 felt that a break of less than 15 minutes was "too short for proper relaxation". I was one of those 43! For me, and the vast majority of teenagers, my brain cannot relax that quickly and, more importantly, when I take a break of that length, the only thing I can think about is:

> *How long do I have until revision starts again?*
>
> Me (during a very short break!)

Therefore, I would recommend that you take breaks of:

- Between 20 and 25 minutes in the morning
- Between 25 and 30 minutes in the afternoon

The exact length of these depends on how long you've just been revising for. Then I would also have a:

- 1 hour lunch break
- 30 minute – 1hour 30 minute exercise break

PRIORITISE

When planning your revision, it is essential that you prioritise subjects and topics according to a number of factors:

1. How long you have until your exam(s) in a subject
2. How good you are at a subject
3. How well you want or need to do in a subject

HOW LONG YOU HAVE

First of all, how much time you spend on subjects must be based on how long you have until your exams. All public examinations take place over the course of 2 or 3 months and must be revised for accordingly. So, if you have one exam at the start of May and another exam at the end of June, you must initially prioritise the one in May, before moving on to spend time revising for the one in June.

As ridiculously blatant as this may sound, many students forget that you'll have study leave throughout the exam period, so you'll be able to revise between exams as well as during school holidays (particularly at Easter). However, once an exam is gone, that's it and there's nothing you can do about it – so make sure you do enough work for the exams you have coming up soonest!

When I did my GCSEs, I had about 2 weeks between my penultimate exam and my final Latin exam. This meant that I could spend a relatively small amount of time revising for this Latin exam during the Easter holidays (30 minutes every 3 or 4 days) and then spend the two weeks of study leave focussing on this exam. Having said that, be careful!!

It is very easy to think: "I've got three days before my last biology exam. I'll leave that until I've finished everything else." However, this is not what I'm telling you to do!

> *Don't completely neglect revision for an exam and leave it all to the last minute.*

The problem with this approach is that, although in three days, doing 6 hours a day, you theoretically have enough time to revise everything you need for your biology exam, you'll never be able to spend that amount of time concentrating on just one subject. You'll realistically only be able to focus for 3 or 4 hours a day. Therefore, it is crucial that you find a balance between prioritising for an exams in the near future and maintaining some revision for subjects in the more distant future.

How good you are

Don't spend more time revising the subjects you like. The chances are that you like a subject because:

- You're good at it and so find it easier than other subjects
- You have a genuine interest in that subject so will revise it more effectively
- You have a teacher you get on with and so learn more in lessons

Therefore, you should actually be spending slightly less time on your favourite subjects and be allocating more time to your weaker ones.

HOW WELL YOU WANT OR NEED TO DO

This third factor is really important and often underestimated. It is particularly relevant to A-level students, but also applies to GCSEs. If you have an offer to study a subject at university, you must prioritise the subjects included in the offer or the subjects which are going to help you meet that offer; if you have a desire to do Engineering at university from the age of 16, the sciences and maths ought to be prioritised over Spanish when it comes to GCSE revision. You get the idea!

THE SYSTEM

This system was showed to me by a friend and is a way of determining how much you need to prioritise each of your subjects in your revision plan. You need to give yourself a predicted grade for each of your subjects that reflects the mark you think you would achieve if you took the exam tomorrow. Base this on any mock exams you've done, your performance in the subject over the year and your sense of how good you are at that subject. It is crucial that you get this right and do not over or under estimate your current ability. If you're really unsure, I would recommend going online and doing a past paper under exam conditions, then using the mark scheme or getting your teacher to mark it. Then write down the grade you want or need to achieve and find the difference between the predicted grade and the desired grade. The higher this value, the more time you must spend revising that subject.

Subject	Predicted	Desired	Difference
Chemistry	A	A*	1
Physics	C	A	2
French	E	B	3

DON'T HAVE LOTS OF DAYS OFF (BY ALEX VAN LEEUWEN)

It is essential that you make the most of your time! You can allow yourself one day off at the start of the holidays and the odd day here and there if your family decides to go on an all-day excursion from 7am until 9pm.

OTHERS NEED TO UNDERSTAND THAT REVISION MUST BE YOUR FOCUS

It is essential that you ensure your parents and friends (especially your girlfriend or boyfriend if you have one) realise that revision must be your focus in the period leading up to your exams. This is not to say that you cannot make plans around your revision (such as a romantic trip to the cinema followed by dinner in the evening), it just means that you need to focus on revision and squeeze in the other things you want to do around it.

YOU CANNOT MAKE UP FOR DAYS OFF

You simply cannot afford to have whole days off on a regular basis; the reason for this is simple, and scientifically proven. As we've already seen, breaks between revision sessions during the day are crucial. Therefore, if you plan to have some days when you do no revision whatsoever and think you'll be able to counteract this with days packed full of work, you'll only be fooling yourself. Each day, you have a set number of hours when your mind is fresh enough to work: for me it is about 5 hours a day. These are what I call 'fresh hours'.

Therefore, if I were to have 3 days away from revision, I would be losing 15 'fresh hours' of revision time – time I simply cannot get back by shoving more revision into another day.

CAPITALISE ON YOUR 'FRESH HOURS'

It is essential that you make the most of these 'fresh hours' when you are in the mood for work as this is when you'll revise most effectively. From my personal experience, people who have lots of days off are usually the people panicking in the week before their exams because they know they could have done more. Admittedly, the people who work everyday during their 'fresh hours' do also panic – everyone worries a bit before exams. However, deep down they *know* that they spent as many of their 'fresh hours' as possible doing highly productive revision.

So, even if you are going somewhere for the day, get up early and do an hour's revision before you leave or do a couple of hours when you get back. Make the most of the hours when you'll be at your most productive and you'll give yourself the best possible chance of success in your exams.

> *Time stays long enough for those who use it.*
>
> Leonardo Da Vinci

REVISE YOUR REVISION

Don't just make revision materials (such as notes, spider diagrams etc.), learn these, test yourself immediately afterwards and then not look at them again before the exam. Plan to come back to topics for short periods of time at regular intervals (maybe twice or three times) during your revision. Test yourself on exactly the same material to check that you remember everything you need to know.

This process of retesting will reinforce the information, ensuring you:

- Know everything needed
- Will be able to recall the information more quickly in the exam room

So, when you plan your revision, make sure you include short sessions for reviewing material you've already revised. This is particularly relevant for learning vocabulary or pieces of information that don't require understanding.

For example, if you revise the structure of red blood cells in Biology, you may understand why they have no nucleus from your first revision session. This is information acquired through understanding the process involved, so *does not* need to be revised again – once it is understood, you shouldn't forget it. However, remembering the exact rate at which red blood cells are produced by the human body (200,000,000,000 red blood cells per day) requires no understanding. This is simply a figure that has to be learnt, so *does* require revising again after you first learn it.

STUDY SMARTER

WHAT'S THIS SECTION ABOUT?

Half of the battle when revising is putting yourself in the right frame-of-mind to ensure that your revision is as productive as possible. The truth is that every single person has things they would prefer to be doing whilst they try to revise! The majority of people will find their mind wanders very easily whilst they are attempting to revise because revision requires mental effort, which does not bring immediate reward; something to which humans are averse.

WHY DON'T WE WANT TO WORK HARD?

We are animals – very advanced animals – but animals nonetheless. As such, our brains have retained an inner chimp, whose sole concerns are for survival and immediate gratification. This part of your brain is called the limbic system and it is what causes us to be naturally lazy, seeking maximum, immediate reward for minimum effort, unable to see beyond the very near future.

WHAT CAN WE DO TO OVERCOME OUR INNER CHIMP?

The answer is twofold. Firstly, we can rise above it, using the rest of our brains (the parts that are far more powerful than a chimp's) to repress our laziness. Secondly, we can feed it, because we'll never be able to totally repress it, by giving it short-term gain when we work hard.

So, it is essential that you realise from the outset that revision is a crucial component of exam success and that, from here, stems a whole host of long-term benefits including: pride, knowledge, a place at college or university and – often most motivational – wealth.

You should also develop a sense of achievement at the end of each revision slot and at the end of each day of revision, acknowledging that you are moving forwards and ultimately bettering yourself. Think of it as a competition: everyone is given the same amount of time to prepare and every moment spent doing nothing when you should be revising is a moment for someone else to get better than you. Take pride in your own ability and know that, no matter how 'clever' or 'stupid' you are perceived to be, anyone can achieve great results, just as anyone can fail if they don't work hard enough. Be determined to expand your knowledge and your chances of future success at every moment during your revision slots, and remember that if you aren't, someone else is!

It's an increasingly competitive world. However, all that means is that you've got to make yourself even better by being positive about your revision and taking a sense of pride in knowing that, when your mum, dad or friend tests you on something, you'll know it all!

The following rules are designed to minimise the difficulty you experience trying to get yourself to concentrate by putting your brain into a 'working mode', which will maximise your efficiency and prevent the following:

"Mum, I'm revising."

You (while you text a friend, watch a YouTube video and scroll through your Facebook newsfeed)

Believe You Can Revise Effectively

> "What's the point? I'm going to fail anyway..."

These are the words of a lazy student who deserves to fail – harsh words, but fair words. The simple fact is that any studying you do will make a difference when it comes to taking tests or exams. Not everything you study will come up on the day of your exam, but if you study effectively (which I'm about to prove you are capable of doing), you're *going* to study important material that *will* appear in your exam.

What is more, I can tell you now that everyone is capable of:

- Revising effectively
- Achieving the grade they want

It may be that you are currently in a very strong or a very weak position to perform well in your exams, but you are, ultimately, able to change that position, for better or for worse!

You must realise that the efficiency of your revision is entirely down to you: you are physically and mentally capable, if you can be bothered, of motivating yourself to revise effectively. Once you've read this book and taken away the techniques and tips for maximising your productivity, it is crucial that you believe you are capable of implementing all of the different elements into your revision.

> *The belief that your revision will be successful is the most powerful tool you have.*

Now, all of this may sound extremely obvious – it is! However, from my experience as a student, the number of people who genuinely believe that they are not capable of revising effectively and that they are somehow less well evolved for revision is staggering.

HOW CAN YOU BELIEVE?

Demonstrate to yourself that you can revise effectively

I distinctly remember that while I was writing my first book, *Exam Grade Booster: GCSE French*, I hit the wall at one point and convinced myself that the challenge of writing a book was far too great. I had completed about 50 pages of the manuscript, but there was no real order to what I was writing and, after an awful lot of effort, I felt as if I had barely begun. However, now that I've completed that first book, writing this seems like far less of a hurdle to cross. Once we've done something for the first time, whether it's juggling or swimming or revising effectively, we gain a belief in our ability to replicate what we've just achieved. So, if you struggle to get through 5 hours of revision without losing your focus, really be determined to succeed in achieving this goal for just one day. Once you've done this, there is absolutely no reason why you can't do it again!

Prove to yourself that your revision works

Do questions (from a textbook or past paper) on a topic before you begin revision and see how many you can answer. Once you've completed your revision of that topic, retry the questions and enjoy the sense of satisfaction and self-belief you gain from seeing that your revision really is effective.

Be inspired by others

Be inspired by others who are driven towards achieving and who have already achieved. Understand that there is no secret ingredient or magic formula behind their success, except perhaps their self-belief!

Prove 'em right (or wrong!)

You need to be able to accept compliments and adopt a positive outlook on your revision. Trust other people's belief in your ability to revise effectively, crediting your friends, teachers or parents when they say that you can apply yourself to your revision and ultimately succeed in your exams. Make sure that you use their positive belief in your ability to improve your own confidence. Equally, if people tell you that you're unable to revise properly and that slacking is in your DNA, be determined to prove these people wrong!

Imagine!

When I'm revising, I create a mental image of myself on results day: I'm happy that I've achieved the grades I wanted. When I lose belief in myself or I'm finding it difficult to find the motivation to revise, I focus on this mental image to ensure that I stay positive and focussed: if I believe in myself and work hard enough, this mental image *will* become reality.

And finally, remember:

> *Whether you think you can, or you think you can't, you're right.*
>
> Henry Ford

Remember: Everyone is in the Same Boat

If you ever say to yourself: "I'm just no good at revising: my brain just doesn't take in the information and I find it so much more difficult to concentrate than everyone else", you are wrong! Revision is tough, there's no point pretending otherwise, but it's the people who battle through it and who realise that everyone is in the same boat when it comes to revising that will perform best. You just have to knuckle down and get on with it, remembering that there are thousands of other people:

- Revising just like you
- Finding it just as difficult to concentrate as you
- Being tempted by distractions such as Facebook like you
- Wanting to stop and just do something else

However, if you are wasting your time being unproductive, giving yourself excuses about your mind not being able to concentrate, there is someone else using their time wisely who *will* beat you in the exam.

If you are insecure, guess what? The rest of the world is, too. Do not overestimate the competition and underestimate yourself. You are better than you think.

T. Harv Eker

Stick to the Plan

Don't be tempted to have an extra hour in bed because it's Sunday, to add another half an hour to your lunch break because you're half way through watching a film or to do some history rather than maths because you dislike the latter!

Once you've made your plan, it is crucial that you stick to it as closely as possible. Of course you also need to be slightly flexible with your revision when necessary (as we saw in Rule 8), but ultimately the vast majority of the time when students don't stick to their plan, it is due to laziness and a desire for instantaneous and easy entertainment rather than the true satisfaction gained from hard work.

So, how can you overcome this natural human desire for easy fulfilment derived from little or no effort?

1. Make your revision fulfilling by splitting it up into small, achievable goals (as in Rule 6).
2. Let your competitive nature fight back! Get into the habit of imagining, whenever you're not revising as you should be, your best friend revising at that very moment and then getting better grades than you come results day. Although this is quite a negative tactic, for many, guilt combined with our natural competitive edge is just what they need to prise themselves away from pleasure and into revision.
3. Imagine success. Right now, build a vivid image in your mind of telling your friends and family on results day about your stellar grades. Feel the sense of pride and opportunity that those grades give you in terms of university, money and

ultimately a better future! Then weigh that against the pitiful satisfaction of playing a game on your phone. Then put the phone down and get revising!

I use all three of these tactics to great effect when I'm struggling to motivate myself to stick to my revision plan. For me (and the vast majority of students), the most difficult aspect of sticking to a revision plan is being disciplined with breaks. Starting work again when my break is over and not saying to myself: "This is a really good episode of *Friends*, I'll just watch another 15 minutes until it finishes" requires a good deal of willpower. However, when I use the three tactics above, I'm able to snap my mind back to the reality that I've seen that episode of *Friends* 6 times before and that I'm going to gain nothing from continued viewing.

I put it into perspective: in a year's time, will I remember these extra 15 minutes watching TV or my exam results?

It is also important to understand that not sticking to your revision plan is a recipe for disaster. Once you let the power of routine slip, you'll begin to fall behind on your revision plan. From here, once you are behind on revision, you'll be less inclined to try to keep up with your plan and the slippery slope towards doing decreasing amounts of revision and ultimately ignoring your plan all together will lurk dangerously close.

Be disciplined, enjoy the satisfaction of completing your revision goals, make the most of your competitive nature and imagine the sweet taste of pride and success!

FIND A HEALTHY STUDY ENVIRONMENT (BY BECKY BROOKS)

Find a fixed place to study (a particular desk or room at home or a spot in the library) that becomes firmly associated in your mind with productive work. All the equipment and materials you need should be within reach, and the room should be well lit and ventilated, but not too comfortable!

It is crucial that you don't use your bed or a sofa as your main place of revision as this will instantly put you in a more relaxed, less focused mind-set. Turn your room into a positive learning environment by keeping books and notes on the desk tidy and looking good – this creates a space in which you are proud to sit and learn.

Another benefit of revising in the same place is that you can decorate your walls with colourful notes and key facts. For example, in preparation for my A-level French exam, I would write key vocabulary on sticky notes and stick them on the wall next to my desk. This meant that every time I looked up from my revision, I could refresh a word or expression in my mind... By the end I had learnt about 150 words like this!

Tip

Having said all this, you may find that revising in different locations for different subjects aids your memory. When you need to recall information, envisaging where you learnt it can be a useful technique. Similarly, you may like to try using sticky notes in different places around your room or house; you may find it useful to envisage the green note on the fridge, for example.

Choose Music Wisely

You may, if you're like me, prefer revising in silence than while listening to music. However, even then, there are times when the right music could improve your concentration. Alternatively, you may be someone who just has to listen to music while you work.

Either way, it is really worthwhile spending a little bit of time finding and then bookmarking or downloading a few good playlists or albums that you can reliably go to when you need music to study to.

I can't listen to music... Why should I read on?

If you like to listen to music while studying, skip this paragraph. So, if you're still here, you'll be comforted to know that I was in exactly the same position as you a couple of months ago. The simple fact was that I thought I really couldn't listen to music while studying, and to be fair, I still prefer to study in silence. However, when my little brother decides he absolutely must be as noisy as he possibly can, or when I'm on the train on the way home from university, or when I'm in the common room, music is preferable to the distraction of other people! The problem you've probably encountered has been that you simply haven't (yet!) found music that you can work to, so read on...

What is the right music to work to?

Frustratingly, there is no one right answer to this question. However, there are certainly wrong answers. You'll need to try different pieces to see what works for you, but in general, the following rules should be followed:

1. No words – you'll read slower if you're also listening to words, and may struggle to read at all (like me; the temptation to sing along is just too much!)
2. No ridiculously heavy beat
3. No excessive bass

Now, you may be an exception and may find that the pumping sound of dance anthems helps you to concentrate, but you probably aren't. The key here is that the music you're listening to helps you to focus; it is not there so that your time spent drifting off can be filled with the music you love.

Personally, my favourite artists to listen to while studying are Sigur Rós (their music does have words, but they are sung in Icelandic or in their own made-up language, so hopefully shouldn't confuse you) and Tycho. However, you can equally find loads of tracks specifically designed to help you concentrate, many of which last for hours, on Youtube, 8tracks, Spotify or anywhere else online.

Tip
If having the Internet available to you (to access YouTube or elsewhere) risks jeopardising your ability to resist distraction, it is probably worthwhile downloading music to play offline.

MAKE YOUR BODY YOUR TEMPLE

You are what you eat. So, just eat all of your textbooks and you'll be fine... Unfortunately not, but your diet is inextricably linked to your ability to concentrate.

DRINK LOADS OF WATER

Drinking plenty of water, either mixed with cordial or on its own, is key to maintaining concentration during revision. Your brain is 85% water. A 1% drop in your brain's hydration decreases your brain's cognitive function by 5%. A 2% drop in hydration means you're likely to suffer from fuzzy short-term memory and has been shown to dramatically reduce levels of concentration. So, just make sure you always have a glass or bottle of water on your desk while you study. Then, drink it. Then, fill it up again!

EAT WELL & EAT OFTEN

Eating a balanced diet has also been shown to improve concentration. Most importantly, try not to eat too many excessively sugary foods (sweets, chocolate etc.) that give you an immediate sugar-rush, instead opting for slower-release carbohydrates (wholemeal bread, crackers, fresh fruit and nuts) that keep you going for longer. You should also try to eat regularly, allowing yourself the occasional treat during your breaks.

> **Tip**
> If you're prone to getting hungry during your revision sessions, having a smoothy on your desk is a great solution.

Sleep

You've probably been told this before, but sleep is a key part of learning and any guide on studying wouldn't really be complete without mentioning it. Sleep is the time when our brains strengthen, consolidate and transform short- and medium-term memories into long-term memories. Revising without sleeping is like spending five hours on a treadmill, before eating three pizzas, two deep-fried sausages and a packet of crisps; all of the hard work you put in on the treadmill is destroyed by eating so much.

Get 8 to 10 hours

So, after a day of revision, you should aim to sleep for between 8 and 10 hours. This length of time is the optimal time for memories to be reinforced, so try to stick within these limits.

Sleep earlier rather than later

Some people claim to be early risers, while others see themselves as night owls. However, when it comes to revision, earlier is definitely better! Studies have found that memories are best consolidated in the hours before 4am, when sleep is generally deepest. As such, maximising the number of hours of sleep you get before 4am will optimise your brain's ability to reinforce memories.

What is more, some of your most productive hours are between 8am and midday, so it's also a good idea to try and be awake for some of that!

KNOW HOW YOU REVISE

This is arguably the most crucial rule in this book and, if there is one thing you should take away from the wealth of advice it contains, it is an understanding of how important getting to know your own style of learning is.

THE SPECTRUM OF LEARNING TECHNIQUES

This chapter has proved to be one of the most challenging to write, purely because there are so many different ways of revising. By the nature of our uniqueness, each individual's brain functions in a slightly different way and, as such, each individual learns differently. In addition, the way in which you revise most effectively may vary quite significantly between different subjects.

As such, it is paramount that I clarify that the sections on different styles of learning that you are about to read are not rigidly defined ways in which the brain works. In fact, you'll find that many of the techniques used in each style overlap with techniques from other styles. What is more, you may find that your brain lies between any number of these styles of learning, so feel free to try to mix and match from any of the techniques put forward.

WHY DID I NEED HELP FROM OTHER STUDENTS TO WRITE THIS?

The apparent problem for me when I set about writing this guide was that I, by the nature of obeying my own rule, know how *I* revise. I've read about different methods from the one I now use and I've tried a few out over the years.

However, I've now developed a method based on my own style of learning that revolves around linear (meaning in straight lines) organisation within my brain, segmenting topics by repeated reading, highlighting and note-making in a bullet-point fashion. This is all well and good, and for around 30% of people reading this guide right now, this method (or a similar one) will work very well. But what about the other 70%? What about the people within that 30% who are also 'visual learners', 'audible learners' or whatever other type of learner?

Obviously, I could not merely set out the way I revise and tell you that is how you should revise too; this would be utterly ridiculous. You must find your own way of revising. As such, I had no choice but to recruit other students (all from Oxford and Cambridge to ensure you receive the very best advice) to offer their own techniques and insights based on their own, very different learning styles.

WHAT ARE THESE DIFFERENT LEARNING STYLES?

Roughly speaking, from all of the people I've spoken to about the ways in which they revise, there emerged two broad modes of setting out and memorising information, each with many, more specific and niche techniques which we'll explore shortly.

> **Note**
> These two broad methods, although different, are in fact united by similar methods of learning. See if you can tell what they are – they should become pretty obvious!

Revision Style	Explanation
Listed Information **(Reading, Writing & Audible Learning)**	Information from a textbook, revision guide or your own notes is condensed into the form of a list. Logical or mathematically minded people often rely more heavily on this method. Information is memorised during the process of condensing information and via the methods below: a. Testing yourself through repeatedly writing out the information, in order, with less and less prompts to help you. b. Testing yourself by speaking to yourself, starting with a topic or an idea and then going through the different details that need to be known within that topic, in a specific order.
Visual Information **(Visual Learning)**	Information from a textbook, revision guide or your own notes is condensed into the form of a mind map, tree diagram or pictorial representation. Creative or artistic people often rely more heavily on this method. Information is memorised during the process of condensing information into diagrams and by testing yourself on the contents of these diagrams.

So, if you haven't worked this out yet, these two different styles of learning are united by two techniques that just so happen (or not!) to form the next two rules of revision: *Condense Everything* and *Test Yourself*. However, before we get onto these, let's go into more detail (provided by a range of students with different revision methods) on how you can enhance your revision by finding the most effective methods of learning for your brain.

Finding what works for you

I would recommend that you try out some of the techniques offered here to see which ones work best for you. Then, once you've found techniques that work, keep using them to maximise your revision efficiency!

LIAM & DAVID'S METHOD — READING, CONDENSING AND TESTING YOURSELF
(BY LIAM PORRITT & DAVID MORRIS)

STEP 1 – READING THROUGH

For a given topic, be it in maths, the sciences or essay-based subjects (the only exception really is languages, so for advice on revising for these, check out pg. 183), the first step of our revision is always to read quickly through our notes and any useful, applicable part of revision guides or textbooks. This is key for two reasons. First of all, it reminds us of the topic itself and of its different constituent parts, instantly giving us an idea of how well we do (or do not!) know the content. Secondly, as we read through each resource, we analyse which parts we think are particularly useful (and which are not) so that we don't waste any time when we begin to make our notes on the topic, paying particular attention to the areas of the topic we don't know very well. When we spot a section that we know we'll find useful or that we don't currently know, we mark or highlight it.

STEP 2, PART 1 – WHAT THE NOTES CONTAIN

Once we've read through the resources at our disposal reasonably quickly, we then begin to target specific areas of that topic, reading through the notes more slowly this time. For maths and the sciences, we'll only make notes on:

- Sections where there is key information that we need to memorise
- Areas with which we are not very familiar

Hence, we don't waste time making condensed notes on something we already know well and fully understand.

The idea is, of course, that the notes we make are condensed. So, for example, we would transform a passage in our biology notes from:

> *Plants, like humans, have a number of fixed characteristics that separate them from other types of organism. It is only when all four of these characteristics are present in an organism that it can be called a 'plant'. Plants are, of course, multicellular organisms, meaning they are comprised of more than a single cell and are always found with cellulose cell walls as well as a cell membrane. Within their cells, chloroplasts allow the plant to photosynthesise, meaning it is able to feed itself, a phenomenon called autotrophic nutrition. Finally, plants are able to store carbohydrates as either starch or sucrose.*

... Into:

> ## Characteristics of Organisms
>
> ### Plants
>
> 1. *Multicellular*
> 2. *Cellulose cell wall (+ membrane)*
> 3. *Chloroplasts – photosynthesis = self-feeding (autotrophic nutrition)*
> 4. *Store carbs as*
>   a. *Starch*
>   b. *Sucrose*

For essay-based subjects, our notes will be much the same. However, in most cases, we'll include information within our notes that we already know as, in these subjects, organising ideas and learning how you'll use them to answer an essay question is as important as actually learning the information itself. For more help on this, have a look at Rule 27 (*Find Ways to Remember what to Remember*) on pg. 105.

Step 2, Part 2 – What the notes look like

As you've just seen in the example biology notes, information is set out in titled lists, according to topic and sub-topic or essay title where applicable. Should you use this method, it is crucial that you write notes for each, individual topic on a fresh sheet of paper, leaving a few lines between each sub-topic, so that you can easily add in any information that you may have missed or that you discover later.

There is often little or no colour on an entire page of our notes, although we often use highlighting or underlining as a means of pointing out key information that may prompt our memory of details. Rather than visual triggers to aid memory, we often use numbered lists, giving a set of information a specific order so that no piece of information is forgotten about. For example, we can easily remember that there are four characteristics of plants and that, if we only have three, we must be missing one.

Step 3, Part 1 – Memorising by testing ourselves aloud for maths and the sciences

We now test ourselves quite simply by covering over (with another piece of paper) the notes, then unveiling a topic title that prompts us to say aloud the appropriate 'answers' or list. So, in the example given, uncovering *Characteristics of Organisms* then *Plants* would prompt us to say the four characteristics of plants. When we've done so, we then uncover the four characteristics to check we're correct, before moving onto the next list. If we're unable to correctly name the four characteristics, we begin testing ourselves from the very start of the notes (on that topic) again, until we've managed

> **Tip**
> We often highlight pieces of information we struggle to recall when testing ourselves. Then, when we come to review our revision later on, we'll only test ourselves on the highlighted parts, instead of wasting time reviewing stuff we already know.

to say aloud all of the information correctly through to the end of the topic. This cycle of repetition when we make an error is not only key to aiding memory, but is also a good way of putting some pressure on our ability to recall the information, as there will be in the exam itself.

When we've done this and are happy we know the entirety of a few topics, we'll then take the notes to our mum, dad or friend and get them to test us again a few days later. Anything we get wrong, we get them to highlight and we learn these pieces of information by testing ourselves on them again. Once we know them, we'll then go back to our mum, dad or friend and get them to test us again.

> *If you've not bothered to test yourself again on the stuff you got wrong, it won't magically float into your brain when you're sat in the exam-room.*

Finally, in addition to this, we'll do past papers to test out our knowledge. We'll then add any mistakes we make in these papers to our lists of information in the appropriate sub-topic (hence why it is crucial to leave lines between each section of your listed notes). Was there a formula you forgot? Did you not know what a certain word or term meant? Put it into your notes and highlight it to make sure you learn it, otherwise you'll end up making the same mistake again! For more information on doing this, have a look at David's advice on doing past papers in Maths and Science subjects, starting on pg. 177.

STEP 3, PART 2 – MEMORISING BY TESTING OURSELVES IN WRITING FOR ESSAY-BASED SUBJECTS

With essay-based subjects, we've found it is best to emulate the way you'll write an essay plan (or ideas for an essay) in the exam room before you actually get there. As such, when we test ourselves on essay-based subjects, we use the 'testing ourselves aloud' method in conjunction with writing out key words in a structured order to produce a skeleton essay plan. Thus, we write down the key words that we need to prompt us to remember the detail. Once we've written a key word, we'll then say aloud all of the detail that accompanies that word, as if we were going to write about it. As before, we highlight any information we forget. We use this method because, for us, the hardest part is remembering what to remember.

This method essentially forms the nuts and bolts of any non-visual revision technique. However, as we've said, a few other nice little techniques can be used in conjunction with this to spice up your revision...

KAT'S PAPER PROMPTER (BY KAT SAVVAS)

This is a simple way of testing yourself and learning shorter terms, answers to questions or key ideas. It works well for a variety of subjects, as it can be used to test yourself on anything from definitions of scientific terms to mathematical equations to translations of foreign words or phrases.

PREPARATION
Firstly, write out some key terms or questions on small pieces of paper (you can cut some up). Then, put all of these into a hat/bag/box/whatever works!

THE GAME
1. Start the game by taking the pieces of paper out of the bag one at a time and testing yourself on the definition or answer. It normally works best if you just say it aloud, but some people may prefer to write it down.

2. Check that what you've said is correct!

3. If you can't answer one, or if you answer it incorrectly, put the piece of paper back into the bag (and maybe give the bag a little shake).

> **Tip**
> Make sure that you cannot see any other answers when you're checking your response. One way to avoid this is by having a duplicate set of all of the terms nearby with the answers written on the back. You can then turn the term over once you've attempted it yourself.

4. Carry on like this until the bag is empty.

5. Repeat this process a few times over a couple of weeks until you can confidently recall the definitions or answers corresponding to each piece of paper.

The ones you keep getting wrong

With a few repeats, you'll start to realise which ones you keep forgetting (and there will usually be one or two that frustratingly fall into this category over and over again). To learn these terms, you can:

- Make a new bag just for them
- Write out multiple copies of these key terms or questions and put them in the bag with all of the other terms so that you'll have to answer them a number of times before the bag is empty.

Time yourself

To make the game more challenging, why not time yourself and try to beat your record each time? Many people find that the time pressure either motivates them or helps them realise where their weaknesses really lie.

How I've used this method

I often use this game for revising vocab in languages and key-terms in science, and found it particularly effective during my GCSE Biology revision, specifically when I used it to revise both terms and questions on the topic of 'Inheritance'.

One reason why this worked so well was that I didn't allow myself to merely quote set phrases or definitions. I had to thoroughly explain terms, such as meiosis and alleles, to myself aloud and in my own words. This led me to notice that there were some terms that, without realising it, I had just been parroting back to myself without completely understanding some of the concepts behind them. This made me go back over my notes, or in a few cases ask teachers, and make sure I fully understood the concept behind the term.

ALEX'S SPLURGE (By Alex van Leeuwen)

This study technique, which requires you to write down everything you know about a specific topic, is one that I use fairly regularly as a way of highlighting the weakest areas of my knowledge. So, here's how it works...

STEP 1
Revise a topic fairly well. This technique is best used when you've already spent some time getting to grips with a topic, learning some of the key ideas, facts, figures, dates, quotes or whatever information it may be.

STEP 2
Try to write everything you can think of related to that topic. With your notes away, splurge all of your ideas onto a blank piece of paper, including any key pieces of information that spring to mind. Try to group ideas together in blocks so that information is next to other related information, but don't worry too much about this.

STEP 3
Compare your splurged notes with your organised revision notes and see what, if anything, you forgot to include. Highlight any bits you got wrong or missed out and make sure you pay particular attention to these sections when you review these notes.

This method picks up on any gaps in your knowledge, and anything you're unlikely to be able to remember on the day of the exam, so you're not like:

"Oh, I completely forgot that America joined World War I. Whoops."

KAT'S METHOD – TURNING NOTES INTO MIND MAPS (BY KAT SAVVAS)

I know a lot of people who struggle with revision because they try to read the same notes that they took in class over and over again, until they 'go in'. However, the whole revision process can be made much easier in one simple step: transforming your notes into something much more 'revision-friendly'. I find detailed notes useful as a starting point, but in order to learn them, I need to condense them, and then condense even more.

> *The aim of this is to categorise ideas repeatedly until just one word can remind you of everything in an entire topic.*

After all, remembering a few key words in an exam is much easier than trying to recall pages upon pages that you attempted, but probably failed, to memorise. One way to put this method to use is by making big mind maps with different colours and font sizes.

STEP 1 – KEY WORDS

In the largest font, in one colour, scatter key words evenly across the page (A4 or A3 for extra space). Then, around each key word, write the main ideas slightly smaller and in a different colour from the first one used for key words. Put the more detailed points in the smallest font,

Tip 🔍
You may wish to use numbers to aid memory. For example, it can help to remember that there are 3 ideas under a certain keyword, and under each of those ideas, there are 5 detailed points.

again using a different colour, around each idea. Of

course, this method isn't limited to just 3 layers, but you should bear in mind that the more layers you use, the less effective this method will be.

STEP 2 – TEST YOURSELF

Once you've made your mind map, have a good look at it and then try to rewrite the mind map without looking, starting from the key words.

> **Tip**
> Use the colours and layout of the page to remember ideas!

STEP 3 – FIND OUT WHAT YOU DON'T KNOW

When finished, compare it with the original and write points you missed out in red or in capitals (or anything that stands out!).

STEP 4 – REPEAT AND REMEMBER!

Then repeat as many times as necessary and at various points throughout your revision period. By the end of this process, you'll only have to be able to remember a handful of keywords, as these will remind you of everything else!

HOW I'VE USED THIS METHOD

I find this method really useful when revising for essay subjects, where giving a Point, Evidence and Explanation (PEE) is key. I used it while revising ideas for an essay on cinematic techniques in *La Haine* for my French A-level. Using layers in the mind map, I could easily include the central categories, then a few points on each category, then a couple of examples for each point. I did not include explanations, however, as it is best to write these on the day of the exam and make them specific to the essay title.

BECKY'S METHOD – USING POSTERS FOR VISUAL MEMORY (BY BECKY BROOKS)

Posters play a key role in my revision strategy as a whole. The way I make posters isn't an exact science. In other words, there's no set pattern that I use for every single poster. In general, I tend to make posters for facts that I need to remember exactly, such as dates or statistics. That way, when I'm walking around my room doing everyday tasks, I can glance at a poster, look at a certain statistic, and say it to myself.

I find that this simple process aids my revision considerably. What is more, having the facts I need to know in a place where I can see them means that I'll definitely get round to sitting down and learning them. It's tempting to make notes of dates and statistics and never consult them again, whereas having them on show in poster form reminds you that they need to be learnt.

PRODUCE FACT-LEARNING POSTERS

Most of the time I'll use a poster as a kind of summary tool. For the majority of topics that I cover in certain subjects (particularly in the sciences), I like to make a 'definitions' poster. For example, this year I made a 'Language Acquisition definitions' poster as part of my linguistics revision. This poster consisted of the terms related to Language Acquisition dotted around on a sheet of A3 paper, alongside their respective definitions.

I find that a definitions poster is a great way of not only learning the meaning of terminology, but also of making you realise which key terms are relevant to which topic. That way, if a key term comes up in an exam question, you instantly have a prepared definition on hand to use either as your answer or, at least, within it. Similarly, if a question comes up on a certain topic, you are already aware of the key terms (and their definitions) that you may need to use in your answer.

MAKE YOUR POSTERS TOPIC-SPECIFIC

I often make posters that address different topics, themes, characters or ideas within a subject or module. For example, at A-Level when I studied *Tess of the d'Urbervilles*, I made a separate poster for each of the main characters. For me, topic posters were helpful as they divided up my revision, enabling me to focus on one topic at a time instead of overwhelming myself with the subject as a whole. In addition, the character posters I used for English Literature were particularly helpful in an essay situation, as I knew I had plenty of detailed points that I could make for each character.

> **Tip**
> The key to my success here was in my ability to make specific points, something that an examiner would certainly have been looking for. You must ensure that you categorise your knowledge rather than merely having a vague understanding of a subject, topic or set-text; precise detail is crucial.

USE COLOUR

It may not sound helpful to have posters that are jam-packed with fact after fact, but I find that the use of different coloured pens spreads out these facts and makes them more manageable. I'll try to use about 4 or 5 different coloured pens per poster, alternating colours for each fact or definition that I write down. That way, I ensure that two facts of the same colour won't appear next to one another. This ensures the facts are well separated and can be remembered individually, instead of merging into one mess of words when you look at the poster.

Even more importantly, the use of different colours means that each fact stands out in its own right and can thus be pictured more easily in an exam situation. For example, you can sit in an exam and think:

> "I know that fact was in orange, and it was in the top right hand corner of the poster."

Without different colours it would be considerably harder to pick out that one specific fact from the many other facts that you learnt from that poster.

USE POSTERS ALONGSIDE PAST PAPERS

I find that posters are also helpful when I start doing past papers. After I've done a paper, I can look immediately at the relevant poster on my wall and see

> **Tip**
> If you don't think you'll be able to resist the temptation of cheating, you may wish to cover up the relevant posters on your walls while you do past papers.

any further points I could have made, or any facts that I may not have got exactly right. Having all the key facts for a topic in an easily accessible place just speeds up the revision process, and avoids the need to waste time trawling through piles of notes.

USE SMALLER 'POSTERS' TOO

When I say 'posters', I don't necessarily always mean elaborate pieces of A3 paper covered in information.

When revising for Maths A-level, for example, I stuck little sticky notes around the house, each of which had a single equation on it. That way, whenever I walked past an equation, I could say it to myself. Equally, I could cover up one half of the equation and test myself on it. I also used this sticky-note method for language revision, sticking up pieces of vocab around the house. Just walking past a word and seeing it helped that word become more memorable.

ASSOCIATE WITH LOCATION

In fact, having these equations and words in specific places in my house meant that I could associate a word or equation with a given location. For example, in an exam I could say to myself:

> "The equation for the area of a cone was on the fridge."

Consequently I would picture my fridge and the sticky note, and try to recall it. For me, having a fact in a location that could be mentally pictured made the fact easier to remember. This little trick has proved to be a real winner for me and I've now been successfully using it for years.

INCLUDE LITTLE PICTURES

I know it's often said that a lot of valuable time can be wasted drawing diagram after diagram on posters – quite often this is very true. Despite this, I firmly believe that a quick drawing can often prove very helpful. I don't mean sitting there and meticulously colouring in some detailed map of the world, because that *is* procrastinating. However, sometimes a little sketch can help reinforce a fact by logging it in your memory alongside some kind of visual trigger.

An example comes from my secondary school history lessons when I learnt about people called 'minstrels'. In order to improve my revision of the minstrels, I would draw little chocolate Minstrels next to the facts about them! The only reason I can still remember anything about minstrels from History is because of this visual aid. The diagrams didn't exactly take long – in this case, it just involved drawing little circles. Yet, they proved very effective...

It was because of these pictures that the facts have stuck in my mind ever since.

In fact, sometimes I found that the act of drawing diagrams was *more* beneficial than just writing out fact after fact. I can still vaguely remember what a plant cell looks like from Biology GCSE because of the diagram I made about it. I didn't spend hours drawing the cell – simply the use of a quick labelled sketch made the facts much more memorable for me.

So when I talk about drawing pictures, I don't mean treating each picture like it's your final piece for Art A-level – just quick sketches here and there can make a poster less daunting and easier to picture in an exam situation.

PIN IT UP

After I've made a poster, it doesn't just go into a pile and get forgotten about – it remains a useful learning tool. I'll pin each poster to my wall, meaning I can come back to them whenever I find a moment. This is a great way of verifying that you know everything you've already revised. For example, with definitions posters, I may test myself by looking at a word, saying its definition, and then checking if I'm correct.

Posters are therefore extremely helpful in reinforcing what you've already covered in your revision – all this stage takes is a few minutes and it'll ensure that, because of the power of repetition, facts are stored in your long-term memory. This stage can also help you work out which topics in a certain subject may need more work, while building your confidence in the topics you do know well.

Tip

If I'm doing something in my room like brushing my teeth or putting on make-up, I can just glance at a poster for a minute or so, and ask myself whether I know everything on it, before then reminding myself of any parts I may have forgotten. Use this method and you will be amazed how many hours of revision you rack up over the course of a couple of weeks.

ALEXIA'S METHOD – TALKING TO HERSELF... A LOT (By Alexia Michaelidou)

This method of revision is particularly well suited to subjects that require memorisation of large amounts of information – examples include law and history – although it could well be applied to pretty much any subject you choose. It essentially uses a combination of visual and verbal/audible memorisation techniques. Although this technique is perhaps less commonly used than others, I find that it is highly effective and more efficient than other, more popular methods.

STEP 1 – MAKE ORGANISED (PRINTED) NOTES

If you're going to use this method of memorisation, you must ensure that you first have a solid set of organised notes.

> **Tip**
> I would recommend obtaining a copy of your syllabus to ensure that you do not leave any sections out. Once you have a syllabus in front of you, you can use the subsections of the syllabus to sort your notes into sections.

Although the vast majority of people find the action of physically writing notes out by hand aids memory, I find this process relatively fruitless when it comes to ensuring I retain the maximum amount of information in the minimum amount of time.

As such, I would in fact recommend that you make use of the word processing tools available to you to make your notes as clear as possible, with the added bonus that you can add and move things around as you go along (something that proves really rather tricky and often very messy with hand-written notes). This includes using headers to clearly mark the beginning of different sections within the modules that you are covering as well as using different fonts, bold text or highlighting to emphasise terms or sentences you believe to be of particular importance.

Producing your notes in this way is not just important for organisation purposes. Colourful headers and the use of different fonts are more memorable. If you find that you are struggling to remember a piece of information later on in the exam, you may be able to trigger your memory by remembering the layout of the page you were revising from.

Keep in mind that you don't need to take this first step too far. The next step of the memorisation process is far more important: as long as your notes are presentable and organised, there is no need to spend hours and hours making them look beautiful. The time that you would spend doing that can be used much more effectively. It is important that you strike the appropriate balance here...

Your notes must be well organised and include visual aids (fonts, bold, highlighting), but should not be unhelpfully over-engineered so that you waste all of your time on this, and run out of time to actually learn the content.

STEP 2 – SPEAKING TO YOURSELF

This is the most important part of this revision technique. Make sure you have the notes described earlier printed out – they could be handwritten if you prefer – and immediately available to you.

> **Tip**
> Sorting them into special revision files can save you time looking for individual pieces of paper later on.

Find a room in which you can be alone and where you are unlikely to disturb others. From here, the memorisation method itself is, in fact, very simple. While the majority of students – or at least the ones I know – use the technique of writing and rewriting information in order to memorise it, I recommend repeatedly saying it to yourself.

Pick up the section you've planned to memorise during the current revision slot and begin to read it aloud to yourself. Personally, I find that walking up and down the room while doing so helps to keep my mind alert. Once you've read a certain amount aloud (3-4 sentences or pointers works for me), look away from your notes and try to repeat them to yourself. It isn't necessary to repeat them exactly as they are written, but make sure that you repeat the gist of the information. If you do not manage to tell yourself the central ideas for that section, read it aloud to yourself again and try again. Continue doing this until you are capable of repeating the information before moving on to the next few sentences or pointers.

Once you've gotten through an entire page in this manner, attempt to repeat the entire page to yourself. Although this may sound a little daunting, you'll probably find that this, in actual fact, comes relatively easily. If you don't manage to remember all of the information, make sure you repeat the sections you've failed to successfully recall a few more times. Proceed through your notes in this manner.

Once you get through the section you've aimed to learn, leave it for a few days and then retest yourself on the whole thing. Go over anything you fail to remember and then test yourself once again. This repetitive process should ensure that everything you need to know is thoroughly lodged in your memory.

THE CRUX OF THIS METHOD

There is one key element in this process that you must use if you want to see the very best results. Earlier, I mentioned that you didn't have to repeat the information you're memorising word-for-word, but that you should instead explain the gist of the information to yourself, giving the central ideas. Another rule in this guide (Rule 31) will emphasise the power of teaching as a method of revising that ensures a deep understanding of the subject matter in question.

So, in a similar vain, as you recall the information using this technique, you must pretend that you are explaining it to an invisible student, imagining

> **Tip**
> Why not think of questions that the imaginary student you are teaching might ask? The chances are that these questions might be similar to the ones an examiner will think of asking.

you are teaching them. I find that using hand gestures and being expressive in the way that I am repeating the information makes this even more effective.

BECKY'S HAND-WRITTEN FLASHCARDS
(BY BECKY BROOKS)

Flashcards are extremely useful because they allow me to easily access the key facts within my revision notes. These "key facts" are statistics, short quotes and definitions that just need to be remembered for an exam, which I'll extract from my notes and jot down onto a flashcard. Having all this key information in one place means that I can easily sit down and commit time to memorising it all.

The process of separating these key facts from all my notes makes the facts seem less overwhelming to learn, and renders them less likely to be forgotten amongst all the other facts.

In addition, having all the key facts in one place on flashcards means

> **Tip**
> Writing key facts onto flashcards is also useful if you only have a quick moment to revise, because you can simply pick up a handful of cards and spend a few minutes testing yourself on them.

that other people can easily test you – a revision technique I find to be extremely helpful. These people will have the facts you need to know clearly in front of them on the cards, and can give you immediate feedback on facts you've missed or perhaps remembered incorrectly.

FLASHCARDS FOR CASE STUDIES
I also find flashcards very useful when revising case studies. Case studies certainly come up a lot in subjects like geography and psychology, and the thought of having to remember them all can be quite daunting! However, you can break down the task by simply using one side of a

flashcard to briefly summarise the key points of a certain study. These points may include:

- The person who undertook the study
- The year of the study
- The methods used
- The results found
- Anything else!!

For me, a brief overview of a study is easily memorisable, and is a much more effective resource than a set of notes that give thousands of details about a particular study in one go. Obviously, as you're revising, you may need to learn some more detailed facts about the case studies. However, the quick summaries are always useful to go back to, as they provide an instant way of ensuring you have the key basics committed to memory.

> **Note**
> This is just an example, but it gives you an idea of the sort of information you should include on your flashcards. I recommend you use a similar bullet point form when you make your own.

ALEXIA'S DIGITAL FLASHCARDS
(BY ALEXIA MICHAELIDOU)

In my opinion, flashcards are an invaluable tool for subjects that require a large amount of memorisation. I've used them for law, history, geography and science, but they can be used for any subject that requires fact retention.

I've never personally used offline flashcards. There are many people who use them very regularly and will tell you they are their most valuable revision tool. I do not dispute that. However, the level of sophistication of flashcard programmes, which offer many more functions than pieces of paper ever could, available for free, online to users today leads me to conclude that digital flashcards are an even more powerful learning tool than their physical brother.

STEP 1 – ASSEMBLE THE INFORMATION YOU NEED
Before you begin producing your flashcards, you need to ensure that all the information you are going to put into them has already been condensed and compiled in one place so that it is readily available to you. Ideally, it should be available to you digitally (have a look at my revision method on pg. 83 to see how I make my notes) so you can copy and paste information directly into your flashcards. If not, you'll have to type the information yourself – not the end of the world as this can itself be a good method of revision.

Remember, you'll want to put a summarised version of the information you need to know into your flashcards.

> *Flashcards are supposed to be short and snappy: you should not be inputting large amounts of text.*

It is easy to get carried away and do this if you are simply copying and pasting information from your notes into the flashcards. However, please avoid this. As a general rule of thumb, they should contain a handful of single-sentence bullet points or up to three sentences. This will help you greatly later on.

STEP 2 – PRODUCE THE FLASHCARDS

There are now a wide variety of flashcard programmes available on the Internet for you to download free of charge. Throughout this guide I'll be referring to the programme Anki simply because it is the programme I use during my revision. However, you may find another programme that is more suited to your revision style or needs.

Once you've downloaded your flashcard programme, I would recommend creating folders for your flashcards according to modules. That way, when you have an exam coming up for a particular module, you'll be able to select to revise only the flashcards relevant to that exam. For example, this year I had a folder for criminal law, civil law, tort law and constitutional law.

Once you have created your folders, you can start inputting information into your flashcards. As you'll already know, flashcards have a very set structure. They have a field on the front and a field on the back. Depending on your subject, you'll use these fields differently. As a law student, I found flashcards particularly useful for cases and legal terms. I would put the name of the case or the legal term on the front of the flash card and the important information about that name or term on the back. This technique will obviously have to be tweaked according to what subject you wish to revise.

Tip
Although this will vary according to what programme you use, if you go with Anki, make sure to select "front and back" when creating your flashcards. This will ensure that the programme tests you by showing you the front of the flashcard, requiring you to recall the information on the back, or vice versa. I found this particularly useful as it allowed me to practice remembering both case names and case summaries, rather than just one or the other.

STEP 3 – REVISE YOUR NEW FLASHCARDS

Now are you are ready to use your new flashcards. If you are using Anki, you'll notice that when you start revising your flashcards, Anki will give you four options every time it presents a card to you – Easy, good, hard, again. According to how difficult you find remembering the piece of information on the flashcard, you should choose an option accordingly. Anki will then use this choice to calculate when it should present the flashcard to you again. If you choose again, this will be a matter of minutes. If you choose easy, it may present it to you again after a number of days. That way, you'll be able to target your revision on exactly the areas where you need it the most.

STEP 4 – GO OVER THEM EVERYDAY

Now that you've produced your flashcards and gone over them at least once, you are ready to incorporate them into your daily revision routine. I use flashcards in combination with

> **Note**
> Anki automatically puts a limit on the number of flashcards you can go over each day. If you notice that your flashcards aren't finished but that Anki isn't bringing them up, this could be why. If you go into settings this limit can be changed. Generally, any questions you have on the programme can be solved by its very helpful website and online user community.

the speaking to myself technique I explained earlier (pg. 83). I would recommend using flashcards in the afternoon when you are more prone to getting distracted. They are an excellent tool to keep you concentrated during periods when you would otherwise find it difficult.

As I said above, Anki will calculate how often it should retest you on each particular flashcard. Everyday, Anki "refreshes" and decides how many cards it'll test you on that day. Once you've finished your revision, ensure that you go through all the flashcards Anki has brought up. This would sometimes take me more than an hour, as I would be going through about 400 flashcards a day. However, in my opinion this time invested is more than worth it. It is an excellent way not only to see what you need to work on more but to actually learn the information you need to learn. In combination with another memorisation technique you find helpful, online flashcards can be a very powerful tool.

Condense Everything

One thing that unites all of the techniques and methods featured in the previous rule (starting on pg. 63) is the necessity for clearly displayed, well ordered information from which to revise. Whatever method of displaying information you choose to use (hand-written notes, printed notes, mind maps, posters or flashcards), the general principle remains the same:

> *Use key terms and visual triggers to spark your memory of more detailed information.*

In Rule 1, we saw the importance of making the very most of the time you spend in class, ensuring you take the best possible class notes as these will form the basis of your revision material. These notes should include everything on the syllabus, although as you make your condensed revision notes, it is worth checking this. However, they are also likely to contain information that is not needed for the exam, including data from science experiments, half-completed worksheets, extra information beyond the syllabus to aid your understanding and more.

As such, you need notes that 'delete' the information that is unnecessary *to you* and 'condense' the information that is necessary *to you*. This is exactly what revision notes are.

> "So, why can't I just use a revision guide then? Won't that have all of the necessary information, ordered and condensed in one place?"

Using Revision Guides

I firmly believe that you can use revision guides to great effect if you use them correctly. Some do indeed contain all of the information you need to know, deleting all of the information you don't – this is exactly what our science guides aim to do!

However, not all revision guides are created equal and so it is definitely worth bearing in mind that the revision guide you are using may not be totally comprehensive. Equally, some revision guides – for example, our GCSE languages guides – may seek to aid you in other ways, such as with exam technique, giving specific advice to enable you to maximise your exam performance, and as such complementing rather than overlapping your class notes.

Yet, if we consider the more traditional revision guide, the key is, as we've seen previously (quite a few times!), that you do more than just read it. Most revision guides of this sort tend to essentially package all of the information on the syllabus inside a single book, thus doing some of the condensing for you. However, there are two problematic constraints when using this sort of revision guide:

> **Note**
> Our Exam Grade Booster science guides contain sections that both help you to test yourself on the information you've learnt and force you to manipulate this information to answer exam-style questions. As such, you are made to revise actively – you simply cannot merely read the guides. They also contain all of the information you need to know in 'Understand' sections.

1. They contain information you already know and therefore don't need to spend time revising. They may also contain some information (from a different exam board) that you don't need to know.
2. The information is unlikely to be displayed in a way such that you find it easy to memorise. It'll almost certainly be presented as bulk text (like in this book), with plenty of visual elements, but lacking the personal triggers that you can add in when making your own revision notes, such as large key words on a mind map or different fonts in printed notes.

What is more, (as obvious as it may sound) the information contained within revision guides is not taught to you by a teacher like your class notes are. The chances are that your teacher explained your class notes to you as you made them during the lesson, giving you the opportunity to ask about any uncertainties you may have had. This means that your class notes are likely to offer a deeper level of understanding than a revision guide.

That said, there may be some elements of your class notes that you struggle to understand. Equally, there may be parts of a revision guide you just can't get your head around. Therefore, there is an obvious solution...

MAKE YOUR OWN REVISION GUIDE

Use all of the resources at your disposal (class notes, revision guides & online material) in conjunction with one another to produce revision notes that *you* will best learn from, drawing on the parts that *you* find most useful. The key is that you only transfer the parts of these resources that you need to revise (i.e. that you don't already know very well) into your own revision guide, cutting out all of the information that you are already comfortable with. However, when you transfer the sections you need to revise, don't merely copy them across as they are displayed in the revision guide, but instead use the methods of presenting information that suit you, from mind maps to listed notes. So, once again (I know I've already said this!):

> *You need notes that 'delete' the information that is unnecessary to you and 'condense' the information that is necessary to you. This is exactly what revision notes are.*

It is the ability to make things personal that renders making your own, condensed revision guide such a powerful tool during the revision process. Just to recap, you should personalise:

Content (I)	Only include information that you don't know very well, excluding anything you are confident you already know well.
Content (II)	Extract content from the resource(s) (class notes, revision guides or online material) that you find most useful.
Style	Use whichever method(s) of displaying information suit your memory

CONDENSE WITHIN YOUR OWN REVISION GUIDE

Once you've managed to put together a guide of your own that includes all of the content you need to revise, displayed in the style you find most helpful, it is a great idea to condense further.

As you begin to learn this content by reading through, highlighting and annotating, as well as by testing yourself (have a look at the next rule on pg. 99 for more information on this), you should begin to try to tick sections off. When you become comfortable with a part of the notes, simply tick next to it so that you don't waste any more time going over this content.

What is more, as you read through these condensed notes (displayed in whatever manner you've chosen), you can highlight or underline key terms. This will then allow you to see these terms at a glance, viewing one of them and then testing yourself on the information that comes with that key term.

WHAT TO DO IF YOUR CLASS NOTES AREN'T UP TO SCRATCH

Unfortunately, it is inevitable that you'll find some teachers' notes and methods suit your style of learning more than others'. However, it is crucial that you take action to combat this. Feeling sorry for yourself won't do you any good, as I'm afraid your exam results won't say anything about how good you thought your teacher was!

If you feel your teachers' notes aren't as helpful as they could be in a particular subject, I would recommend using a revision guide to help you. With any luck, once you've cleared up most of your areas of confusion and ensured your revision will cover everything on the syllabus, you should be able to ask another teacher at your school to help you.

> **Tip**
> It is also a good idea to have a look through the syllabus online to ensure that you are familiar with everything on it. If you find parts you don't think your notes cover, make sure that you find another resource from which to revise that section.

It is also definitely worthwhile searching online for resources to help you with topics you struggle to understand, as there is some really great stuff out there (some of our favourite resources are listed starting on pg. 115). However, you should also be aware that anyone can publish content on the Internet, so any information you find there should be checked against information on other, ideally more reliable sites (such as Wikipedia – now generally pretty trustworthy).

Regardless of which resource (revision guide, teacher or online) you use to overcome your substandard class notes, you should, as we've already established, use this to create content for your own 'revision guide', including only the material you don't know very well, presented in the style you think you'll find most helpful.

So, in the end, you really *can* make up for unhelpful class notes; you are just going to have to work extra hard to do so!

TEST YOURSELF

So, hopefully the rule we covered from pg. 63, *Know How You Revise*, has given you a reasonable idea of the distinct but overlapping styles of learning favoured by different students, as well as some innovative techniques that you can use during your own revision. However, these really are only a handful of ways (all be them very effective ones) used by a few people I know; there are loads more and you should feel free to come up with your own, personal ways of revising.

Regardless of your personal preference when it comes to displaying information, the best way to make sure you know all of the information included in your notes, spider diagrams, voice recordings or whatever else you may like to use is to test yourself. It is also wise to get someone else – a family member or friend – to test you too.

However, for now, the key idea to take away is that, when trying to memorise information, the mere act of reading it to yourself in your head is extremely unlikely to make the information sink in. In fact, it's actually a sure-fire route to boredom within about 20 minutes of your revision slot. Instead, you should be making your notes in whatever form works for you and using the techniques from the *Know How You Revise* rule, or your own methods, to test yourself on the information.

Testing yourself is the only way to build confidence in what you do know, while highlighting the areas you don't know.

UNDERSTAND WHAT YOU REVISE

Isn't it tempting to pass over a piece of information that you don't understand? When you see something that doesn't make sense to you, you instantly and automatically begin trying to understand it. However, the problem arises when this process fails to make sense of the information. The amount of effort required to then find out what is going on is often the reason why students leave gaps in their understanding of topics. For example, if you were marking a Maths past paper you had just completed and there was a particular process required to complete a question which you cannot understand by looking at the mark scheme, it requires a relatively large amount of effort to get hold of your teacher who will be able to explain it to you. At this moment, you would probably decide that the chances of that technique coming up in the paper you take are very small and so you would decide to move onto the next question. DO NOT DO THIS! By ensuring you fully understand every small piece of information you come across during your revision process, you can make sure that you avoid thinking the following in your exam:

> "You've got to be kidding me! This is the only tiny part that I don't understand.

Secondly, don't be too embarrassed to ask your teacher about something you don't understand – even if you have to ask more than once. I almost made this mistake this year in my Further Maths A-level exam. While doing a past paper I had come across something that I didn't understand. It was a relatively small and insignificant part of the largest topic on the syllabus. However, I made sure to ask my teacher about the question when I next saw him and he explained it to me. The problem was that I did not really understand his explanation and so nodded along, pretending I knew exactly what was going on. I was embarrassed to admit that I didn't understand something that everyone else in the class seemed to find incredibly straightforward. Fortunately, one of my classmates put up his hand and asked our teacher to explain it more carefully until he (and I) understood it. In my exam, there was a question worth over 10% on this exact topic. Had I been alone with my teacher, I would have lost all 10% of those marks due to my pride and refusal to admit that I didn't understand something.

Why do you need to understand what you revise?

1. As much as you can learn facts off by heart (something that has to be done during revision), sometimes learning information superficially and without true understanding will mean that you cannot apply a concept to different contexts, as required by a specific exam question. During exams, you must answer 'the question, the whole question and nothing but the question' and a lack of understanding will limit your capacity to manipulate your knowledge to suit a specific exam question.

2. The simple fact is that knowledge that is understood and that can be placed into the context of your understanding is far more memorable than random pieces of information.

Make Facts Relatable

So, the previous rule will allow you to learn information that you can place within the context of your understanding. However, you still have the problem of trying to remember individual facts.

> *If a fact means nothing to you, you won't remember it.*
>
> Ed Cooke, Grand Master of Memory

The key to revising information is to relate what you're revising to something you already know. Memories don't just form in your mind separately of one another; they build a web of memories linked together and if you can control what a memory is connected to, you have a far better chance of being able to recall it later. You need to take personal memories and create vivid images, memorable sounds or distinctive ideas in order to allow you to remember a random fact, a piece of vocab or a technical definition. These memory links are known as mems.

Use mems

So, how can you make up your own mems to help you remember facts? Simple – just come up with a sentence, a line from a song or an image which you mould to ensure you don't forget a piece of information.

For example, in latin, *tamen* means *however*. So, in my mind I imagine I'm sat in a restaurant and the waiters come over and give me my steak and chips. I say "Ta *(as in thank you!)*, men. However, the steak is a little overdone." Here, I'm simply forming a sentence combined with the creation of a vivid scene in my mind that allows me to remember an otherwise abstract piece of vocab.

Create vivid images

Similarly, if you wanted to remember that the Battle of Britain happened in 1940, I would imagine that my friend called Georgie Britain was born at twenty to eight (19:40 on a twenty-four hour clock). Or, if I wanted to remember that, in physics, drag is the force that pulls objects backwards, I would create an image of a man in drag (in a dress) pulling me back while I'm walking along a street.

Use rhyming words

Just as you can use words that have two different meanings (such as *drag*) to create mems, you can also use words that rhyme. These are most useful when trying to remember vocabulary for foreign languages, such as the Spanish word *aterrizar* meaning *to land* in English. To learn this, I remember the sentence 'I like to land at Terry's bar!' This doesn't make much sense and the instant image that comes to mind is of a plane crashing into the roof of a bar. This is perfect as it is very memorable and combined with the rhyme between *at Terry's bar* and *aterrizar* forms a brilliant mem that I won't forget anytime soon!

Sing it!

Another way to remember information is to adapt song lyrics to suit what you want to remember. I often combine these lyrics with an image because it's pretty hard to come up with lyrics that fit! People make up entire songs to help them revise, or you can simply change one line. For example, if you wanted to remember that a *champignon* in French is a *mushroom* in English, I imagine Freddie Mercury (*Queen*'s lead singer) with a mushroom hat on singing: "We are the champignons of the world!" (From the song *'We are the Champions'*.) Slightly more inventively, if you want to remember that the capital of Saudi Arabia is Riyadh, you could imagine Amy Winehouse singing: "They tried to make me go to Riyadh, and I Saudi no, no, no!"

Turn numbers into words

Finally, one really neat technique that you may find useful if you are trying to remember specific figures is to convert the digits of these figures into words. This involves creating a phrase in which the number of letters in each word corresponds to a digit. So, you can remember the value of pi (3.1415926) by memorising: "May I have a large container of coffee?" The only problem with this technique is the number '0' because no words have zero letters! This can be solved by using a word that starts with a 'z' to correspond with '0' instead.

Summary – Look for:

- Words that have two different meanings (e.g. *drag* or *tamen*)
- Words that sound similar to one another (e.g. *said* and *Saudi*)
- Words that rhyme (e.g. *aterrizar* and *at Terry's bar*)
- Vivid and memorable images (e.g. a friend's birth!)
- Ways to turn the completely abstract (e.g. a date) into something personal (e.g. the time of an event)
- Numbers (e.g. pi) to turn into a sentence

FIND WAYS TO REMEMBER WHAT TO REMEMBER

It's easy to miss out whole chunks of information that you've learnt simply because you forget the information exists, not because you forget the details of that information. For example, if I've learnt ideas for a paragraph on the inevitability of fate as a theme within Shakespeare's *Romeo and Juliet*, but forget that this idea even exists in the exam.

Equally, finding yourself, mid-way through an exam, struggling to remember a specific piece of information can cost you dearly. For example, imagine you are sitting in an English exam and have learnt a set of 10 quotes from *Romeo and Julliet*. You are half way through a paragraph and decide that you need to include a quotation to support your argument. However, to your horror, you have a complete mind-blank and cannot remember the quote you've learnt that relates to what you are writing about. You then sit there for five minutes, panicking, unable to continue your essay until you remember the quotation.

Under the pressure of exams, it is very easy to draw a blank on specific pieces of information. Once this happens, you are left in a pretty dangerous position: your overwhelming natural reaction is to begin panicking, thus wasting crucial time. Therefore, you need to first of all realise that, if you do forget a piece of information, you're not the first (and you won't be the last!) person to do so. Stay calm and don't spend more than about 30 seconds trying to remember the piece of information. Either find a way around the problem (for example by using a different quotation) or move on, leaving sufficient space for you to come back and complete the answer or paragraph once you've remembered the quotation. The chances are that once you move on, you'll calm back down, your mind-blank will clear and you'll be able to remember the information you were after.

However, in an ideal world, you would not forget the piece of information in the first place! Undoubtedly the best method to 'remember what to remember' is to use mnemonics. This relies on the fact that you know the information well and that therefore, if you were to have the first word or even letter, you could remember the whole quote or fact.

Use mnemonics

Mnemonics act as memory aids in a way that allows personalisation and creativity. They use the first words or letters of pieces of information to form sentences that should be easy to remember. The best-known mnemonic is for the colours of the rainbow – 'Richard Of York Gave Battle In Vain'. You can devise many more of these to aid your personalised recall of pieces of information across all of the subjects you study. For essay subjects, this is useful in remembering key points in an essay plan. Equally, it can be used in other subjects, often to recall something that needs to be given in a particular order. For example, in Maths, to remember which of SIN, COS and TAN I needed to use when presented with opposite and adjacent angles, I remembered the mnemonic: 'Some Of Hugh's Class Are Having Trouble Obtaining Angles!' Or, in physics, to remember the order of the planets I used: 'My Very Eccentric Mother Just Shot Uncle Norbert' and to this day I can still tell you the order of the planets is: Mercury, Venus, Earth, Mars, Jupiter, Saturn, Uranus and Neptune!

Avoid Distractions

Distractions during revision are amazing:

- Your parents think you're revising
- You fool yourself into thinking you've spent hours working really hard when, in fact, most of the time was spent being distracted
- You are provided with immediate satisfaction in return for absolutely no effort whatsoever

Hmm... Distractions are your worst enemy when you're trying to revise. Unfortunately, the art of procrastination is something that the vast majority of students master fairly quickly. In fact, according to research conducted in 2007 by Piers Steel, almost 50% of university students procrastinate so much that it causes them problems – and I reckon this figure translates pretty well across students of all ages.

The main problem is that humans naturally seek to avoid effort and to gain short-term pleasure – our inner chimp again! The ease with which I can fulfil my desire for instant gratification by simply stopping revision, unlocking my iPhone and beginning to scroll through my Facebook or Instagram Newsfeed is just far too tempting.

Is there a solution?

The simple answer is yes!

In fact, there are a few solutions that I now use in combination to great effect. I like to think that this is the real benefit of my writing this book as a student for other students: I've faced this problem to quite an extreme degree, just like many other students, but I've found a way to overcome it that can be applied by anyone.

REVISION:

THE ACT

OF TEXTING, WATCHING YOUTUBE, EATING,

SCROLLING THROUGH INSTAGRAM

AND HUMMING

TO MUSIC WITH

A TEXTBOOK NEARBY

My story

For me, the temptation to procrastinate during revision slots was by far the most worrying cause of inefficient revision. I am incredibly determined, which is generally a positive thing when it comes to concentrating, but with this comes a susceptibility to becoming very obsessive.

With the surge in popularity of social media sites, my desire to write books and loads of other distractions to prevent me from studying, I found myself, during the Easter holidays prior to my A-levels, unable to resist looking for ways to market my books, unable to resist keeping up-to-date with what was going on in the world of social media and unable to resist playing games on my iPad – Clash of Clans was a particular culprit.

The ease with which I could access all of these distractions, my slight complacency following good results the previous year and my inability to relax totally during breaks was wreaking havoc with my productivity.

Not using breaks wisely

During breaks I was spending the whole time at my desk counting how many new likes my Facebook page had received (feel free to give it a like – we also have a great Instagram page that is sure to motivate rather than distract you). As such, I was not allowing my mind to rest or my desire for instant gratification to be fulfilled.

Solutions...

Use your willpower when you need it, otherwise allow it to be replenished. Willpower, on the face of it, does not seem to be a disposable resource for human beings (although I suppose the energy required for us to use our willpower is – but let's ignore that!) and so, theoretically, you are capable of overcoming all distractions, without needing to allow your willpower to be replenished. However, in reality, as we go on through the day, willpower to fight against distractions dwindles. Therefore, it is crucial that, during your breaks, you allow yourself to be rewarded with doing things that you enjoy. Like this, you allow your mind and willpower to relax and give yourself the best possible chance of maintaining focus during your revision slots.

> **Tip**
> This is why, in the afternoon, you should work for slightly shorter periods. You should also do less draining tasks, such as answering past paper questions instead of making revision notes.

For more information on using breaks wisely, have a look at the next rule starting on pg. 113, *During Breaks, Get Out*.

LOOKING AT MY PHONE DURING REVISION SLOTS

During revision slots, I would keep track of how long I had been working using my phone. This seems like a reasonable idea; I use my phone as a watch all the time when I'm out and about.

However, the problem was that my phone was just sat there. The temptation to have a look at it every time the screen lit up was overwhelming! Even if I managed to overcome this temptation, there was an even bigger one: whenever I wanted to see what the time was, I would physically have to press a button on my phone. Suddenly, I was looking right at a load of notifications and, almost without even meaning to, I would unlock the phone and check them out. Autopilot would set in and 10 minutes later I would still be scrolling through Instagram photos until I realised (eventually!) that I should have been revising.

SOLUTIONS...

The simplest way to prevent yourself from becoming distracted is quite simply to turn off all electronic

Tip
Use a physical timer (watch or clock) rather than your phone to time revision sessions.

devices (your laptop, phone and tablet) for the duration of each revision slot. This method is by far the best as, with electronic devices turned on, it is easy to tap on an app or open a web page and become instantaneously absorbed by this distraction, rendering you unaware of the fact you are even supposed to be revising. By contrast, if it takes 30 seconds for you to access a distraction because it is turned off, your brain will be able to use this waiting time to become conscious of the fact you should be revising, and rather than being swept away instantly, your rational mind should find it far easier to return to revision.

If you can't bring yourself to turn devices off completely, airplane mode is a great solution to prevent notifications from popping up and distracting you.

However, this won't work if you want to use technology as part of your revision (for example when revising languages to look up vocabulary). Even still, there are a few great ways to ensure you steer clear of distractions!

Airplane Mode	If you can use an app on your phone or tablet offline, airplane mode is definitely the best solution.
Sign Out	Signing out of your favourite social networking sites is another great method as it works in a similar way to switching everything off. If you have to spend time consciously logging in, your rational mind will hopefully kick in and alert you to the fact that you should be revising!
Website Blockers	These sites allow you to prevent yourself from accessing specified sites for specified periods of time. Cold Turkey and FocalFilter are the two best website blockers around, so if you can't resist looking at Facebook, they could be the solution for you.

Turn Off Notifications

If you need to use the internet, the main cause of distraction will be notifications that pop up while you are working. For example, while looking up a piece of vocabulary, I would often be tempted to tap on a notification that popped up at the top of the screen. Simply turning off notifications for the apps that most distract you (Facebook, Twitter, Instagram etc.) is a great way to prevent this. I also actually find this a great source of motivation, as I know that when my revision slot finishes, I'll be able to discover what notifications I've received (as sad as that sounds)!

Delete Apps

This is what I had to do during my A-levels when 'Clash of Clans' was taking over my life!

Willpower

Perhaps easier said than done, try to use your willpower to resist temptation. I find it particularly helpful to imagine my friends working hard whenever I reach for my phone; my competitiveness kicks in and I get back to it!

Hopefully you'll be able to apply some of these techniques to great effect, preventing technological procrastination from taking over your revision sessions. However, as we'll see shortly on pg. 115, you can actually do far more with technology than just ignore it. You can make technology your friend.

DURING BREAKS, GET OUT

So, the previous rule told you that breaks are a key time when your willpower can be replenished and your mind can totally relax. Remember that this is your mind's reward for achieving its goal during your most recent revision slot.

This is all true, but there are also a few things you can do during breaks that will further improve your attention when you recommence revision. The most important thing is that you leave the desk or room where you are working and go somewhere else, thus physically exiting the focused work zone and entering another space that you associate with relaxation.

In my opinion, one of your breaks should be dedicated to exercise of some kind. This break can, if you want it to, be longer than an 'ordinary' break. Exercise has been scientifically proven (in a test carried out on over 1,000 Aberdeen schoolchildren, published in the journal *Developmental Medicine and Child Neurology*) to improve concentration levels. This exercise does not have to be overly rigorous and could include:

- Walking the dog for half an hour
- Going for a jog or run
- Doing some sit-ups, press-ups, ski-sits etc. in the garden or your room
- Going on a bike ride

This is just a handful of simple suggestions that the vast majority of people should be able to implement!

What about the other breaks? The simple fact is that, as tempting as it is to spend breaks between revision playing video games or on Facebook, you'll work far more effectively after your break if you go outside or at least leave the room or desk at which you are sat.

If you revise at your desk, then go on Facebook at your desk, then play a game on your iPad at your desk, then try to work again at your desk... The work simply won't happen. In no time, your ruler will be coloured in and you'll be thinking about anything and everything, except the revision you're supposed to be thinking about.

The problem for many students trying to revise is that, during breaks, they don't allow the part of the brain used during revision to switch off. For example, if you've just finished reading through notes and testing yourself on them and then decide to go onto the Daily Mail website to read the latest gossip, your brain is having to work in a very similar manner, reading and processing information. Therefore, after your break, your mind is no more ready to work than it would have been without a break!

Therefore, you need to change the way your brain is working during your breaks. For me, talking really helps – interaction and conversation with other people takes my mind away from revision and also provides the brain with a totally different kind of stimulation. Similarly, going downstairs and watching some trash TV means that my mind is far more relaxed, but also processing a completely different type of information. Going outside for a quick sunbathe, baking cakes, kicking a ball against a wall or giving your friend a call are great ways to spend your breaks and will ensure that you are ready to recommence revision once your break is over.

Make Technology your Friend

As we saw previously on pg. 107, technology can be an incredibly disruptive force during revision. That said, it can also be an amazing tool that allows you to revise in a more interactive way, keeping your mind focused and speeding up the revision process. For me, I currently see technology as a great way of complementing other, more traditional study methods – although, it is worth adding that, as technological resources and apps improve, I think they will play an increasingly important role in education.

I am not going to give a very comprehensive overview of the resources available to you online as the fact is there are loads of great ones out there, all of which can be found pretty easy by googling whatever you are after. Instead, I'm going to run you through a few golden nuggets of tech that you can use yourself, hopefully giving you a few ideas as to how you can incorporate them into your own revision.

Use YouTube

For a long time, YouTube has been and will remain one of the strongest contenders for best all-round revision aid. The reason for this is quite simple:

There is a video for virtually every part of every topic on every syllabus in every country... all for free!

If you're struggling to understand something in maths or science, you can look up an explanation. If you're studying Shakespeare's *A Midsummer Night's Dream*, why not watch an actual performance of it? If you're feeling tired one afternoon and want to do some work on Spanish, watch a news episode in the language. If you're studying woodwork, find out how to make a rocking horse... You get the picture – or should I say the video! (Sorry – I couldn't resist!)

Test yourself online

Flashcards – Anki (By Alexia Michaelidou)

I find that digital flashcards are a particularly effective way of testing myself. Digital flashcards can be produced online or on the variety of free programmes available to be downloaded – Anki is the one that I use and wholeheartedly recommend. These programmes are designed specifically to test you on the flashcards that you have the most difficulty answering.

For example, if you take ten seconds to find the answer to one flashcard (or don't manage to find the answer at all) and only two seconds to find the answer to another, the programme will process this information and proceed to test you more often on the cards you had difficulty answering. This is an excellent way to ensure that you are targeting your time and effort on the sections where it is most needed.

Quizzes – Quizlet

Quizlet is another great little site and app that does exactly what it says on the tin: quizzes! It allows you to produce your own quizzes, great for definitions, vocab, quotes and much more. It also allows you to search for and access other people's quizzes.

Make online mind maps – IHMC Cmap Tools (by Becky Brooks)

I generally prefer to make my own, hand-written mind maps, but I do occasionally like to mix up my revision by using an online program to produce a visually appealing resource and, in my opinion, this downloadable software is by far and away the most easy to use and most effective.

Other sites we love

I'm only going to give you a few as I really don't want to overwhelm you with loads of suggestions that you just ignore, so here are a few that we rely on...

- Literature – SparkNotes
  SparkNotes (online & app) is an absolute lifesaver when it comes to offering in-depth summaries of literary texts. It also has sections on key themes, characters and quotations. It won't give you everything you need to write high quality essays, but it is a great way of checking you've understood exactly what is happening and what is of importance in a book.

- Languages – WordReference
  WordReference (online & app) is simply the best online language dictionary.

- Maths, Science & Programming – Khan Academy
  Khan Academy (online & app) is a free resource offering loads of great video tutorials and tests.

TEACH & LEARN OUTSIDE THE CLASSROOM (BY JOE TYLER)

I mentioned the idea of having a 'study buddy' in the first rule in this book (pg. 19). I suggested discussing topics and questions with your friends or teachers as a way of really cementing your understanding. Here, I'll really dig into the power of teaching, and learning from, a study buddy.

> *Teaching is the most effective way of learning.*

BOUNCE IDEAS AROUND

I would suggest revising as a pair or in a group of no more than four, as this provides you with discussion partners who can give other opinions and angles without the session turning into a shouting-match as everyone tries to put their point across.

HOW IT WORKS

For me, working in conjunction with a study buddy was brilliant in the early stages of the revision process.

STEP 1
Listen as the information is explained to you in class and take good notes.

STEP 2
Revise it, making condensed revision notes (of some kind).

Step 3

Teach it to yourself, going through the key points you'll explain to your friends and thinking of any questions they may ask.

Step 4

Teach it to others in order to test your ability to explain the information in a concise manner under a little bit of pressure. Allow your study buddies to take notes as you teach them and make sure you ask one another questions.

Then, we'd go away, revise another topic each before teaching one another again in our next session.

Flash-Teaching to Refresh Your Memory

However, there was one key part of our revision session that we would always start with. We would begin by taking it in turns to briefly teach each of the topics we'd covered so far, ensuring that the teacher this time hadn't taught that topic in the previous session.

During this flash-teaching period, the new teacher (who had been taught the material in a previous session) was expected to cover the key points and also to ask the others questions to ensure they had remembered everything.

> **Tip**
> We often turned this into a game, either as a quiz, or timing the teacher to see how long it took to teach us all of the key points in a way that we understood, deducting marks for any information missed out.

Discuss Past Paper Questions

You may find, particularly in essay-based subjects, that discussions with study buddies are most productive when you focus on a specific question. This is a great way of exposing yourself to different ways of approaching questions and you can openly discuss the best ideas and examples to use for that specific question.

> **Tip**
> This method generally works best if you plan answers to questions before you have a revision session with your study buddy or buddies so that you have already given it some thought before trying to discuss it.

You should also try discussing various permutations of questions around the topic. There is a big difference between knowing the answer to a certain question and having the understanding to answer any question on the topic. It is unlikely that exact questions you've practised will come up so having the ability to adapt your answers is vital.

WHY IS THIS METHOD SO POWERFUL?

In my experience people often dismiss their own difficulty in explaining things to others by claiming that it makes sense in their own head, usually to shield themselves from the truth that they don't have a good understanding of the topic. Do not underestimate the importance of being able to explain something verbally.

If you can't clearly and concisely explain a topic to someone you know in a relaxed atmosphere with no time pressure, what makes you think you'll do better in the stressful and time-pressured environment of the exam?

This isn't to say you should lose hope if at first you struggle to explain things clearly because it'll take time to adapt, but it is important to realise that examiners want clear and concise answers and will reward you for them, so it is worth taking time to practice this skill.

DO PAST PAPERS PROPERLY (BY LIAM PORRITT & JOE TYLER)

Practicing past papers is one of the most useful and important forms of revision at your disposal. Done correctly, it can greatly improve your chances of success in exams. However, so often students use past papers incorrectly and don't get the most out of them.

PAST PAPERS ARE JUST LIKE DIVING

Imagine you dream of becoming an internationally acclaimed diver, Tom Daley style. Fundamentally, all you need to be able to do to dive is: jump, move and swim. This is similar to the core knowledge needed in exams provided to you by revision. However, you have to be able to turn these core abilities into something that will be marked highly by the judges (or examiners).

This means practicing diving over and over again, learning to manipulate your body (or knowledge) in ways that will score you marks. However, you would not begin practice from the 10-meter platform (that's really quite high when you get to the top of it!), but instead start at the bottom on the poolside and work your way up gradually. Practicing for exams is exactly the same (except slightly less terrifying).

START GENTLY
You should begin by doing a couple of practice papers (from your exam board) with your notes to help you, taking your time to work through them carefully. If you get stuck, take a look at the mark scheme (although it is crucial you don't just copy it out – this does you no good at all) and try to understand why you didn't know the answer to a

question. Make a note of the topics you struggle with so that you can go away and revise them again more thoroughly.

Get tougher on yourself
Then, build up to doing a practice paper, still taking as long as necessary, but now only using your notes to help you when you get stuck. Then, you can begin to do them under timed conditions, first of all with notes, then in proper exam conditions. When you do papers under timed conditions, it is imperative that you are honest and finish when the time is up. If you don't, you'll be lulling yourself into a false sense of security; come the exams you won't be able to give yourself an extra minute to finish an essay!

Don't be disturbed

It is essential that you are not disturbed while doing a past paper. Make sure you tell your family that you'll be busy doing a paper for the next couple of hours so that they don't ask you to help doing the washing up half way through. (We reckon this is a nice bonus that comes from revising and working hard – parents generally expect less in terms of household chores!)

Do papers in the right format

Finally, if possible, make sure that you are practicing papers in the same format to the one you'll be taking. Occasionally, if you are the first year to do an exam after syllabus changes or exam restructuring, you won't be able to do a past paper in exactly the same format as the exam you'll be sitting. However, even in this case, the exam board will release sample papers for you to do.

Familiarity with a paper's structure will mean that you are far less likely to miss sections out or struggle to finish because you'll have a far better idea of how long each section will take you. This should allow you to gauge how quickly or slowly you need to work, preventing both unnecessary rushing and costly slowness.

> **Tip**
> Knowing the paper's format will also mean that you're familiar with any question choices you may have to make. Do you only have to answer a certain number of questions? Will you have options to choose from? What sorts of questions will you be able to choose? What sorts of questions would you most like to choose?

BE AS TOUGH AS YOU CAN BE

If you're marking your own past paper, be critical of your work. You gain nothing from self-leniency. If your teacher marks the paper, ask to go through the paper with them.

Having completed the past paper and highlighted the areas for improvement, consciously force yourself to incorporate those changes into the next past paper you do. You may find there are habits you've fallen into that are regularly criticised by markers; for example, going off on tangents, failing to maintain a clear essay structure or forgetting to include units in your answer. Make a list of these and keep them in your mind every time you do a past paper; eventually you'll train yourself out of these bad habits and into ones examiners love to see!

If you've already addressed these habits before you sit the exam, you'll have one less thing to worry about, allowing you to focus on the content of your answers.

DON'T FEAR BEING WRONG

Quite simply: being wrong is how you learn! If you are too afraid to ask your teacher for help when you don't understand something, it is entirely possible that the something you don't understand will appear in your exam!

However, even more importantly, when it comes to answering questions or doing past papers as part of your revision, it is crucial that you don't leave questions out without attempting them. During revision, students tend to leave questions out because:

- They don't think they'll be able to work out the answer for themselves
- They simply can't be bothered to try when there is a chance they'll get the question wrong

However, it is by answering incorrectly (or maybe even deducing the correct method for yourself!) that you'll gain most from doing questions and practice papers. For example, if I were to do a maths practice paper and, whenever I

> **Tip**
> We all make mistakes and, having discussed it amongst the ten of us, we all believe that a large part of our success is down to trying things out and learning from our mistakes. We also agree that we struggled much more in subjects when we lacked the confidence to try things out. So, don't be afraid to give it a go!

couldn't do something, simply looked in the mark scheme and copied down what it said was the right method and answer, I would learn very little because my brain is simply copying information without giving it much thought.

If, by contrast, I attempted the question incorrectly and then, while marking the paper, spent time to look at and understand the method offered in the mark scheme, my long-term memory would record the information, allowing me to remember exactly how I should approach questions like this one in the future.

> *The moral is clear: invest some time in trying things out, which may mean failing occasionally, if you want to maximise learning in the long run.*
>
> Tom Stafford, The Guardian

Actually Revise

This is an appropriate place to end this section on studying smarter.

I'm delighted you're taking the time to read this guide, and don't doubt that it is going to have a profoundly positive impact on your studying habits.

> *However, don't spend too much time reading books about revision!*

While they *will* improve your efficiency during revision and *will* hopefully increase your levels of motivation, they *will not* help you in your exams at all if you don't spend time getting on with your revision.

Once you've learnt how to plan, study smarter, optimise exam performance and get the most out of each and every subject, you really must start revising, rather than spending any more of your valuable time learning how to revise.

Optimise Exam Performance

What's this section about?

There is nothing more frustrating than putting in hours and hours of hard work over the course of an entire year, then spending hours and hours revising all of that hard work, to then flunk your exam because your exam technique is poor or because you capitulate under the pressure of the exam room.

This section is specifically designed to target every part of the exam period. It will:

- Help you to manage stress and anxiety before exams
- Instruct you how to spend time between exams
- Provide you with loads of tips and tricks that you can use in the exams to ensure you make the most of your potential under pressure

Having spoken to loads of students, drawn on my own experience and looked at a ton of studies, it has become clear to me that the greatest issue for students during the exam period is excessive, negative anxiety.

One study has found that out of 13,000 students, 96% have experienced exam anxiety, so if this is a problem for you, you are not alone! However, the issue is that highly anxious people were shown to perform 12% worse than those who were slightly anxious, or not anxious at all.

So, as we wrote this guide, we really kept that in mind, trying to put a greater emphasis on stress management.

NO ALL-NIGHTERS

We've all watched TV shows that portray teenagers struggling to work for a test, staying up all night in the hope that they will be able to counteract their total lack of effort throughout the year with one night of study. As Will from *The Inbetweeners* found out, his colour-coded schedule that jammed work into every second of every day and his caffeine-fuelled studying through the night did little to improve his hopes of exam success!

What was more, his all-nighters (as well as his daily 8 cans of energy drink) had a profoundly negative impact on his physical well being, leading to frank disaster on the day of his exam. This is hilarious to watch, largely because it is not that far from the truth; all-nighters put your mind and body under immense pressure that ultimately leads to inferior exam performance.

In fact, studies have shown that reasoning and memory are negatively affected for up to 4 days following prolonged nocturnal studying. By contrast:

Memory recall and ability to maintain concentration are much improved when an individual is rested. By preparing early and being able to better recall what you have studied, your ability to perform well in exams is increased.

Dr Philip Alapat (Medical Director, Harris Health Sleep Disorders Centre)

Don't Burn Out

What does 'burning out' mean?

It means that you peak early and then perform poorly in your exams because you've been overloading your time with revision sessions (and possibly other commitments) that demand too much of your mind and body.

So, what might you do that could cause you to burn out?

- Study too hard, too early during the revision period
- Study non-stop throughout the exam period
- Do nothing but study
- Study when your body is telling you not to
- Not get enough, high-quality sleep

Fortunately, there are a few rules that you can follow to prevent you from burning out, ensuring that you peak when it matters most.

Crescendo

The worst-case scenario is that you burn out before you even get to your exams. I've heard of plenty of people revising for 8 hours a day (although I wonder how many of these 8 hours were spent procrastinating in their bedroom – remember we need to work smarter as well as harder!) during the first few weeks of their revision. Then, with two weeks to go until their exams, they've burnt out. They simply cannot sit at their desk for more than about thirty minutes without wanting to rip up every piece of paper on it!

So, you need to crescendo (build up) your workload over your revision period. You can afford to be a little more relaxed with five weeks to go until the start of your exams. If a friend invites you over for the afternoon, feel free to go ahead! Although I am certainly not saying that you should do this everyday, you really can afford to have some time off at this stage.

However, as you get closer and closer to your exams, you should be a little tougher on yourself, ensuring that you make the most of the crucial time in the two to three weeks prior to your exams.

DURING YOUR EXAMS, RELAX YOUR STUDYING

This may sound crazy, but from all the people I've spoken to, the general consensus was that a fair bit of time between exams should be spent relaxing!

> *If you don't know it all by now, you won't know it all by tomorrow.*

That said, the power of short-term memory should not be underestimated. The afternoon and evening before an exam, going over and testing yourself on everything you've covered can prove an extremely powerful tool.

What is more important, however, is your physical and mental state on the day of the exam. As such, allowing yourself a little more time to relax during the course of your exams is key. Your revision should continue, and your study sessions should remain focused, but the amount of work your give yourself should be reduced.

How much should you revise?

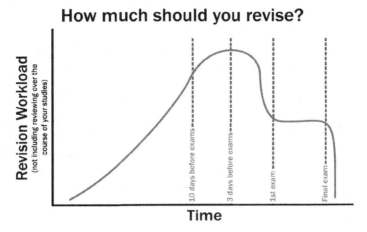

This graph gives a rough guide as to what your revision workload might look like in the run-up to your exams. Notice that it crescendos up until about three days before the start of your exams. At this point, it relaxes a touch down to a stable level that should be maintained throughout the course of your exams.

DO OTHER STUFF

This rule is fairly self-explanatory. Essentially, I really want to get across that, if you've worked smart and you've worked hard during the course of your revision, you can afford to see friends, watch TV and get out! Obviously don't go out and get no sleep. Obviously don't spend all day every day chilling on the sofa.

> **Tip**
> Make sure that you exercise! Not only is exercise a great way to distract yourself from the pressures of exams, it has been scientifically proven to improve academic performance and also means that you sleep better, another key component in the equation for exam success.

But do allow yourself some time to take your mind off of revision and exams.

KNOW WHEN TO REVISE HARD... AND WHEN TO TAKE A BREAK

If you're feeling tired or unfocused, trying to plough on with revision, especially during the exam period, will wear your mind and body down. Over time, refusing to listen to your own body when it tells you it is overtired or overworked leads to less focused and less motivated study. Not only will it mean that the time you spend revising will be far less effective than it otherwise could be, it could also mean that you are unable to concentrate and perform to the best of your ability when it comes to your exams.

The solution is simple:

> *Listen to your body and be honest with yourself.*

Why is being honest with yourself so important? Only you can distinguish between when you are genuinely tired or just feeling lazy. Then, you either need to take a break or confront your laziness.

Similarly, if you're feeling particularly tired while working of an evening, be honest with yourself and feel free to stop. Chill out for half an hour and then get a good night's sleep so that you wake up refreshed and ready for a productive day's studying.

PMA

Positive Mental Attitude! This has to go down as arguably the most important rule in this entire book. The simple fact is that your exam performance relies on three factors:

1. How hard you work
2. How smart you work
3. How much you believe in your ability to succeed

This third factor is perhaps the most disconcerting; surely you have little power to control how confident you are in your own ability? You either are or are not a confident person.

It's a two-way street

Well, this is not entirely true. First and foremost, I want you to understand that growing confidence is a two-way street: study more effectively, and your confidence will grow; grow in confidence and you'll study more effectively.

Be realistically positive

Secondly, you must be realistically positive. That is to say that you must be positive in your hopes and aspirations, but that these positive goals must be realistic *for you.* If you are dyslexic, or really genuinely struggle with writing, be positive that you can make the most of your situation, but don't expect to be able to learn how to spell every word in the English language within a week!

Okay, so now we have established a few basic ground rules for being positive about your studies, how can you overcome your fears, reduce your anxiety and generally see exams in a more positive light?

CONSIDER EXAMS AS OPPORTUNITIES FOR SUCCESS

This may sound like a ridiculously idealistic view, but it is one you should really consider adopting as it actually holds more truth than you might think.

Exams really are designed as an opportunity to show what you know, not as an obstacle designed to trip you up. Education systems are built as positive institutions that are designed to teach you and then give you an opportunity to demonstrate, to yourself and the rest of society, how much you've learnt.

When examiners mark exams, you're awarded marks for what you know, not deducted marks for what you don't!

You aren't expected to know everything. However, you are expected to work your hardest in the run-up to your exams so that you can show the examiner your very best work. He or she is then able to award you with the best grade you could possibly have achieved.

IMAGINE THE SUCCESSFUL VERSION OF YOURSELF

While staying realistic, you should get into the habit of imagining what you'll look like and how you'll feel when you achieve your goals. Looking at yourself in the mirror and telling yourself you can achieve your goals (and really meaning it!) has also been proven to increase confidence and reduce anxiety.

Write your worries down

This can be a really powerful technique for converting negative concerns into positive solutions. Here's how it works:

Step 1 – Get your worries out

Sometimes half of the problem may be that you're not being totally honest with yourself, ignoring the fact that you have concerns about your exams. Equally, you may be trying to block your worries out completely.

This is not the way to deal with anxieties. You need to be open with yourself about any concerns you may have *before* you can face up to them. So, take out a blank piece of paper and write down any worries you may have about your exams in general, about specific subjects or anything else that you think may affect your exam performance. Ensure you leave a reasonably big gap between each concern.

Step 2 – Come up with solutions

While admitting that you have concerns is a very positive step, it is even better if you can consciously seek ways to combat these concerns. So, for each one of your worries, come up with a way you are going to solve that problem. For example, I might write down the following:

Worry: I might run out of time in my English exam and not write very much for the last question.

Solution: I'll keep a close eye on the clock and ensure I stick strictly to spending 25 minutes on each question, so that I have 10 minutes left at the end for checking.

Step 3 – Throw it away!

Once you've admitted to and found a solution for each of your concerns, screw up your piece (or pieces if you're particularly concerned!) of paper and throw it in the bin.

BEWARE OF POST-EXAM ANALYSIS

It is almost impossible to abstain from the exam post-mortem, so I'm not going to say that you shouldn't discuss answers briefly with your friends. However, as a general rule, 5 minutes after the exam is over, stop thinking about it all together and move on.

> *The golfer, Tiger Woods, when he was at his peak, spoke of the 'Tiger 9 steps'. He would allow himself 9 steps to be angry after he messed up. Then he would block it out and concentrate on the next hole.*

The reason for this is simple: the more you think and talk about your exam, the more you're likely to find you answered questions differently from other people and the more disheartened you'll probably become.

Just because you did something differently from someone else does not mean you're wrong. You could both be right. Or you could be right and they could be wrong. And even if you were wrong, you'll have got stuff right that other people got wrong. But, more relevantly, talking about it is utterly pointless because you can't change what has happened. Ultimately, you need to focus on the exams that lie ahead, not the exam you've just done.

CONTROL STRESS... AND THEN EMBRACE IT

WHY DO WE GET STRESSED?

When you are threatened, your body releases stress hormones, such as adrenaline and cortisol, helping you to stay alive in a fight-or-flight situation.

Stress is a powerful tool that helps us get motivated to do things. However, it can also be dangerous, particularly in an exam situation, as it ups your heart rate, blood pressure and blood sugar, which can cause you to feel panicked. This sensation may mean that you find it difficult to focus on exam questions and can also make you feel sick or dizzy.

HOW STRESSED SHOULD WE BE?

There is a fine balance between being so relaxed that you lack the motivation to do anything and being so stressed you become extremely unproductive. Last year, I really did find this balance difficult and I ended up getting extremely stressed about my end of year university exams, so I understand just how hard it can be to keep stress under control. In theory, this is how it works...

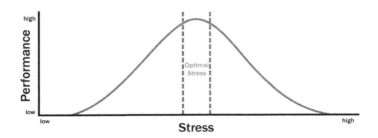

Now, you may be thinking that it is all well and good to say that you should maintain stress in the 'Optimal Stress' zone, but how can you actually do that?

I'm afraid that this section really isn't designed for people who find they are too relaxed; hopefully the rest of the book will be able to motivate you to get cracking! Instead, these recommendations are designed for people who struggle to control their stress levels in the run-up to their exams.

Have 'downtime' as 'downtime'

For me, one of my biggest problems was that I was unable to switch off from my exams. I felt guilty every time I would go and play football or chill out with my friends or watch TV: it felt as though I was wasting time that I could have been using to revise!

However, since then, I've worked out a great way to overcome this feeling of guilt by changing the way I view downtime. Instead of as a waste of time, I see it as an important part of the formula for achieving success and as something that will make me more productive when I return to studying. Of course, this does not mean that you should spend all of your time doing nothing because 'it's an important part of the formula for achieving success'. However, when you have breaks in your schedule or if you have an afternoon off, really try to put studying out of your mind and just have fun, seeing this time as an important tool to make you more efficient while you study.

Question yourself

A lot of people consider questioning yourself to be negative, saying you should always believe in yourself and ignore any negative thoughts you may have. However, questioning yourself and being honest with yourself is one of the most powerful tools for controlling stress. Of course everyone has their own causes of stress in the lead up to exams, but these are the sorts of questions that I find really useful in controlling my stress levels and staying positive:

> "Why am I likely to fail?"
> "What can I do to change that?"
> "What good is that attitude going to do me?"
> "What's the worst that can happen... really?!"
> "Am I concentrating on my weaknesses and neglecting my strengths?"
> "What is the point in getting wound up like this?"
> "Am I expecting myself to be perfect?"

The key to making this work is ensuring that you consciously look for times when you are feeling panicked or stressed, and then ask yourself questions like these to put things into perspective and really ensure you address the causes of your stress, rather than allowing them to fester inside you.

REMEMBER THAT EXAMS ARE NOT THE BE-ALL AND END-ALL

It may sound like something your grandparents would tell you and that you'd ignore as ridiculous, but it really is true. If you follow the advice in this book, it really is very unlikely that you'll fail. However, if you were to fail, it isn't the end of the world; I know loads of people at some of the best universities in the world who have, at some point, failed exams. They all recovered, learnt from it and went on to succeed in retakes or in subsequent exams.

Strike a powerful pose

It has been scientifically proven that standing in front of the mirror in a way that exudes confidence, with your hands on your hips and your chest out (in your best Superman impression) for just 30 seconds reduces stress and increases performance.

Meditate

I certainly don't claim to be a mindfulness expert, but I've recently taken to spending 5 minutes every so often 'in the moment'. If you knew me, you would know that I'm one of the world's most sceptical and to-the-point people, so please don't think that I happily accepted 'breathing slowly' as a method of reducing stress without testing it myself.

However, I genuinely do believe that 'meditation' is a great way to reduce stress. I use two techniques that allow me to completely distance myself from all of my thoughts, concentrating only on what is happening right at this moment:

1. Breathe in for 7 counts, out for 11. Once you establish a rhythm, stop counting, and concentrate on the sensation of your lungs expanding and contracting for 5 minutes.
2. While walking alone, focus on a particular sense. For example, feel each part of your foot as it touches the ground with each step you make, or

listen very closely to every sound that you can hear.

Embrace stress

Perhaps most importantly, I encourage you to embrace stress as a positive force that helps, rather than hinders you. Hopefully next time you feel your heart pounding and you have a slightly queasy stomach, as you sit there waiting to start your exam, you'll remember reading this and you'll think to yourself:

> "This is my body's way of helping me overcome this challenge."

So, you really need to start seeing stress as a tool. If you make stress your friend, it then becomes what scientists call 'eustress' (the positive type of stress) as opposed to 'distress'.

When I've been talking about 'controlling stress', that really meant 'controlling distress'. If you can combine these two approaches, firstly controlling distress, and then viewing your remaining stress as a positive force to help you, you'll become more productive and, ultimately, more successful.

Get Everything Sorted in Advance

Taking exams is a stressful experience for anyone and you are inevitably going to feel a little on edge in the days and hours in the run-up to your exams. However, you should do everything in your power to ensure that, in the hours before the exam, you feel in control and comfortable with exactly what is going to happen up until your exam starts.

Take a trip to your exam room

It's definitely a good idea to make sure you know exactly where your exam room is well in advance of your exams. You should also be aware that your exams won't necessarily all be in the same place, so be sure to check out each of the exam rooms you'll be using. I also strongly recommend that you go inside the room when you go to visit it. It may sound strange, but this familiarity is actually very comforting when you are sat in a room full of people about to take an exam.

Sort your bits and bobs

Pencil Case
You'll need to make sure you have your pencil case equipped with everything you'll need before the morning of your exam. Be aware that you may need a clear pencil case, or may not be allowed to take in a pencil case at all. Make sure you have a couple of sharpened pencils and be aware that in some countries you have to write in black ink. Don't leave this stuff to the last minute, as that is sure to stress you out on the morning of your exam.

WATER BOTTLE

If you think you'd like to take a water bottle with you to the exam, it's a good idea to get a clear bottle with no labels well in advance.

CANDIDATE NUMBER

For pretty much any exam you take now, you'll almost certainly need some form of candidate number or identification code, so it's a good idea to memorise yours, or at least ensure you have it written down somewhere safe before the morning of your exam.

GET UP & GO

I definitely recommend having a routine for the morning before your exams. Set an alarm to wake you up so that you have plenty of time to get yourself ready and to your exam room well in advance of the exam. If you get there early, you can always go for a walk to calm your nerves.

Do not be in a rush.

EAT, DRINK, SLEEP

The night before your exam, try to relax. Do some revision until a cut-off time (I usually set this at 7pm) and then have a shower, watch some TV, have a good meal, drink plenty of water and then read before going to bed early. If you can't get to sleep or are jumpy, don't panic. I promise you that everyone has had a bad night's sleep before an exam: the adrenaline will keep you going if you need it to! Aim for 8-10 hours, but don't worry if you get less, just lie there and imagine how amazing it'll feel when all your exams are over!

AVOID CHOKING

> *He was shot. He was choking, bottling, yipping, bricking, cracking, call it what you will – and there was no way out.*
>
> Matthew Syed (author of *Bounce*)

The sensation that you are choking, cracking under the pressure of one of the most important events of your life, is awful and, as pointed out by Syed, inescapable. If only you could make it stop, getting back to normality and performing as you have done over and over again during practice. But you can't. There's nothing you can do.

Perhaps you've felt this before in an interview or playing football or singing a solo or maybe in an exam. You've sat down and suddenly your mind has gone blank to everything and you just sit there. The more you try to recall information you've learned and revised, the more you panic and the more you feel like you know nothing.

You're wasting time! Then, eventually, maybe you think of something, and it all starts coming back. But you've just wasted 15 minutes and now you're behind and rushing and you're never going to get the grade you deserve.

WHY DO PEOPLE CHOKE?

You may, or may not, have learnt to drive. You have, however, at least got in the car and been asked by mum or dad or whoever is picking you up: "How was your day today?" As you were asked that question, mum or dad or whoever began to drive off, without really thinking about what they were doing, focused on asking you a question rather than on the actual process of driving. They are in 'autopilot' mode. Their brain is using what is called its 'implicit system', which works as a result of hours and hours of practice, so that their body drives the car, without really needing to think about it.

To start with, when you learn to drive, you have to consciously think about the precise movements your body is making, using your brain's 'explicit system'. It is only once you begin to repeat the actions involved in driving a car over and over again that driving becomes automatic.

Similarly, when you begin your revision, you systematically learn information, consciously making an effort to understand and get to grips with the information, using your explicit system. However, after time, you begin to be able to recall information automatically, without really thinking about it. When you hear a certain question, your brain automatically produces an answer for you, using your implicit system.

However, under the pressure of the exam, you want to succeed so badly that your explicit system completely overrides your implicit system. During exams, you need to use both systems in conjunction. The implicit system is needed to recall information you have stored within your brain, picking up on key words in the question and automatically providing the correct material. Your explicit system is needed to consciously decide which information is needed to answer the specific question in front of you, rather than merely writing down all of the related information you have memorised.

However, when you choke, you try to consciously come up with the information that your implicit system would normally supply for you automatically. Under the pressure, you try to think, rather than allowing the information to just appear – you try too hard! This is what people call 'having a blank'.

What can you do to prevent choking?

Tell your mind it means nothing

Before sporting events, it is common for athletes to tell themselves 'it is only sport'. Instead of thinking about the importance of the event in which they are about to participate, they think of everything that is more important to them: health, happiness, family, relationships. You can do the same. As we saw previously in the rule to help you control stress (pg. 139), realising that exams are not the be-all and end-all is key to maximising performance.

Here, even more than that, the belief that the exam you are about to take is critical is potentially going to cause you to choke. Instead, replacing this belief in the minutes before the exam with the thought that it does not really matter should disable the tendency for your explicit system to override your implicit system for the first few questions of the exam. And once you are on your way, there's no stopping you.

Think happy thoughts

Before your exam, have a few happy visualisations that you practice conjuring while studying. Then you should, if you feel like you are choking, just be able to draw on them for 10 seconds to calm yourself down.

Earn Marks Shrewdly
(By Nat Trueman)

Liam used an analogy in his introduction to this guide that is very relevant here: you should see yourself as a shrewd businessman or woman, but one who deals in marks rather than money.

Make the most of every second

> *The shrewd businessman makes the most of every second he has at his disposal, and finds time other people didn't even know existed. The shrewd student acts similarly.*

When you sit down in the exam room, don't waste time. You'll have at least 5 minutes waiting time, which you are given to read the instructions and write your details. You should have already read the instructions on one of the several past papers you completed as part of your revision, and writing your details won't take very long.

So, that gives you plenty of time that shouldn't be wasted sitting there, twiddling your thumbs. You want to start to focus so that when the exam begins you can get straight into it. To give you an idea, during this waiting time, I like to think about formulas and ideas, going over some of the information that I've memorised for the exam. I find it useful to have already recalled some of the information in the exam room during this waiting time, as, for me, this minimises the chances of blanking out once the exam has begun.

If you get lucky, you can even be a little sneaky and read some of the questions through the front page, without actually turning it over. This way you can start thinking of all the possible ways you could tackle that first question before the exam has even started!

> **Tip**
> For science and maths, I often memorise all of the formulae in a particular order before the start of the exam so that I can quickly jot them all down in pencil somewhere as soon as the exam starts. Liam agrees that a similar technique can be used in foreign language exams with phrases or in literature exams with quotations.

RAKE IN THE EASY MARKS FIRST

> *The shrewd businessman doesn't waste his energy trying to earn $10 when he can earn $100 elsewhere in the same amount of time. Only once he has made the $100 will he target the $10. The shrewd student acts similarly.*

Make sure you never leave out questions you could have answered with ease. Mismanaging your time in the exam can easily cost you a full grade if you try to answer the hardest parts of questions before ensuring you've completed all of the easy questions. The biggest exam 'crime' is to leave out questions that you knew the answers to. Look at it like this: *it is much easier to get the first 80% of the marks for any question than the last 20%.* Therefore, if you find that time is slipping away as you tread water on your fourth answer out of six, don't spend your remaining time struggling on with that question, or perhaps (even more foolishly!) extending and perfecting that answer. Instead, move on to questions five and six and make sure you get the key ideas, arguments, formulae or calculations written down for any parts of questions you find easy.

Always keep in mind that, if you've answered only three questions out of six, failing to do the fourth question and spending all of the remaining time on it, the highest mark you can get is 50%.

MAKE A START

The shrewd businessman doesn't give up because a task is slightly unfamiliar. He instead manipulates his prior experience to fit the task at hand. The shrewd student acts similarly.

If you don't know where to start on a question, write down what you know. Write down anything related to the question, and it should spark ideas and help you remember things. Try to remember questions you've done that are similar to this as most exam questions are just adaptations of questions from past papers. However, examiners are not stupid and they often disguise them to try to throw you off. Don't let this fool you and make sure you don't give up as soon as you see a question you're not sure how to answer.

Make the examiner's life easy

> *The shrewd businessman does everything in his power to please his customer. The shrewd student acts similarly.*

Another thing that I always remember when writing my answers is that there'll be a person marking the exam. Making their job as easy as possible could well help you gain marks. I always show my answers clearly by underlining or circling the final answer and by always writing my answers line by line and not in a mess with different parts scattered all over the page. This not only makes it more straightforward for the examiner to mark, but also makes it easier for you, working through in a structured manner.

Know when you're struggling and do something about it

> *The shrewd businessman knows his own capabilities and acts accordingly. The shrewd student acts similarly.*

Since most people are used to revising with frequent breaks it can sometimes be difficult to maintain focus for the whole exam, especially if the exam is 2 or 3 hours long. During one of my A-level exams, I hit a brick wall and started to lose concentration and panic. So I went to the toilet, had some water and just took a minute to clear my head. When I got back in I was able to focus so much more and saved what was going to be a really bad exam.

Yeah, I lost a few minutes but I would have lost a lot more time panicking.

Use the process of elimination on multiple choice questions

The shrewd businessman evaluates his options. He then makes a snappy decision by sifting out the impossible choices on offer. The shrewd student acts similarly.

For multiple-choice questions, it is a good idea to read through all of the answers and cross out the ones that are definitely incorrect before selecting the answer you think is right.

If you are unsure of an answer, this is the best method to use as it narrows down your options and increases the likelihood of your giving the correct answer. However, ensure that, if you whittle it down to one of two, and you are really not sure which one to go for, you don't spend too long trying to decide which one to go for. Go with your gut and move on.

In the worst case scenario that you have no idea what the answer is or you're running out of time, definitely make a guess: never leave a question blank! Try to make this a smart guess – often 2 of the answers are very similar and the others are completely different. For example, in a maths question, two of them may be different by a factor of 10. It is likely that the exam writer put this nearly correct answer (out by a factor of 10) as an option because it's very easy to make that mistake. Therefore it's very likely that the answer is one of those two. Now the guessing has reduced to a 50/50 chance of getting it right.

Have a quick check when you finish a question

> The shrewd businessman has an eye for detail and always checks his work before handing it over to a client. The shrewd student acts similarly.

Looking back at the question once you've completed it is a great habit to get into. Have you answered the question that was asked? For numerical answers check that it looks like the correct order of magnitude. For example if you're working out the speed of a car and you're answer is 700mph, you're probably wrong. Use your judgment and common sense.

Mark grab when the clock is ticking

> The shrewd businessman knows that he may have to scrape the barrel for a few more dollars. The shrewd student acts similarly.

As you near the end of the exam, you may have some questions still left to answer, which you either left out because you found them tricky or you haven't yet got onto. At this stage, I've had it where I've been so pushed for time that I just wrote down key words or formulas really quickly in all the blanks.

This is a great way to try and scrape a few extra marks and could be the difference between a B and an A. Don't come to the end of the exam and think:

> "I've only got 1 minute left. There's nothing more I can do."

Scribble in anything you think might earn you a mark as quickly as you can. From looking at mark schemes, you'll have noticed that a lot of them are in note form, asking to see certain words or certain formulas used. If the exam marker sees these key elements, even if not as part of a complete answer, you are likely to earn some of the marks available for that question.

ANSWER THE QUESTION

Not answering the question is a fatal error that will mean you score very few or maybe even no marks at all on a question. Here's how to make sure you do as you're told!

READ THE QUESTION CAREFULLY

According to examiners, one of the most common errors they come across is giving what is known as a *triggered answer*. By not reading the whole question carefully, students write down a pre-learnt answer to a question without actually establishing what information the question is asking for. As such, they write down the wrong information.

DON'T MISS A QUESTION

In the heat of the exam, it is all too easy to miss a part of a question that is over the page, or to miss an option for a question that, had you seen it, you would have answered. Make sure you are familiar with the paper and take a little more time during your exam to ensure you don't make this kind of potentially disastrous error.

> *Your CV won't be able to say: "I should have got an A, but I missed out a question so got a C."*

In my university exams this year, I did exactly what I'm telling you not to do. I hadn't taken enough time to ensure I knew the exact structure of the paper beforehand. As such, I didn't see the essay title on my preferred topic and had to write an essay on a topic I didn't know as well.

Rule 42: Answer the Question

Look how many marks are available and be concise

If a question is worth one mark, a single sentence or maybe even a single word will suffice. Don't waste time writing more than is necessary as this will not only mean you have less time to answer other questions, it will also mean that the examiner is unsure whether you really know the answer, or if you are just writing down information you've learnt in the hope that some of it is correct.

Don't repeat yourself or include any information that may be deemed irrelevant; this is likely to annoy the examiner and result in a lower mark.

Don't try and pull the wool over the examiner's eyes

By this, I mean don't try and play sneaky tricks to fool the examiner: they almost certainly won't work! For example, writing two answers for a one mark question and kind of crossing them out, leaving it uncertain which one is your final answer. If there is any doubt, the examiner will mark your answer as incorrect.

Similarly, if you are unsure of a quotation or aren't quite sure how to do a calculation, but try and fudge it in the hope that the examiner won't notice, it is very unlikely to work! If you are unsure of an exact quotation, don't include it. If you aren't certain how to do a calculation, write down all of your working and show the examiner you were almost there, but not quite; at least then you'll be awarded marks for your working.

Subject-Specific Advice

WHAT'S THIS SECTION ABOUT?

This section does exactly what it says on the tin, providing you with specific advice you can implement in both the revision process and the exams themselves. It takes you through the key techniques involved in essay-based subjects, science and maths, and languages. Each section is written by students who specialise in each subject area and who have a wealth of experience to share with you.

So, without further ado, let's crack on with this final section. Obviously only read the sections that apply to you. Enjoy!

ESSAY-BASED SUBJECTS
PART I : REVISION (By Cameron Anderson)

When it comes to revising for essay-based exams, students generally seem less sure of where to start. This in itself is not surprising. These subjects rely on the individual conjuring relevant ideas or arguments, and maintaining them for long periods of time, without the aid of an exact mark scheme or syllabus that tells you whether you are right or wrong. Students who don't take naturally to writing can often feel overwhelmed, and struggle to structure and apply what they've been taught over the course of the year in their exams. However, revising and sitting these exams can be made far easier if you learn how to master two basic components of essay revision:

1) **Essay content**
2) **Essay technique**

One frequent mistake students often make is to forget one of these components, most commonly essay technique.

Whilst learning content is a necessity if you want to write a successful essay, equally important is knowing exactly how to structure and mould this content.

Over the course of the next few pages you'll learn how to effectively revise these two components, and then you'll be taught how to utilise what you've learnt during your revision in an exam.

ESSAY CONTENT

Too often is it said that "you can't revise for English," or "you can't really revise for essay questions." This is absolute rubbish, as you are about to find out...

KNOW YOUR STUFF!

Knowing the fundamentals of the course you're studying is essential. This content forms the building blocks with which you'll build any essay. You simply can't write about World War I without knowing the key dates of battles or about Macbeth without knowing the plot. This might sound obvious, but noting and learning by heart key details must form the basis of your revision; any skirting around specifics will be picked up by an examiner and will cost you dearly.

Consequently, making quality revision notes is the first step to exam success. There are a number of techniques not specific to essay-based subjects earlier on in this guide (pg. 63). However, here are some of my tips and tricks, specifically for essay-based subjects.

NOTE MAKING

When making notes, condense key quotations, dates, or case studies into memorable points, by way of bullet points, flashcards, mind maps, or any other technique you may like to use. When doing this, there are a couple of things to be careful of:

LIFT ACCURATELY

Firstly, make sure you are careful to lift content, which can be taken from textbooks, class notes, books or any other resources, accurately. There is no point in learning a quotation incorrectly, as this will cost you – rather than earn you – marks.

> *3rd July 1777*
>
> *'To be, or not? That is the question'*
>
> *Wolfgang Amadayus Mozzart*

... Writing this sort of thing (giving incorrect dates, quotations and names) is only going to give the examiner the impression that you don't really know what you're talking about.

> **Tip**
> To avoid misspelling names in your exam, ensure that you have learnt how they are written out during your revision. If you like to speak to yourself during your revision or frequently test yourself aloud, it is wise to ensure that you make sure you know how to spell any tricky names of people or places.

PICK RELEVANT & SPECIFIC CONTENT

Secondly, make sure that the content you pick out for your notes is relevant and specific to the section of the subject you are revising, such as *The reasons for the start of World War I* or *The character of Oberon in 'A Midsummer Night's Dream'*.

For English Literature, I would recommend that you make notes on your text chapter-by-chapter, summarising the story and noting down key quotes. Alternatively or additionally, you may find it helpful to make notes on individual characters. For History, I find it helpful to develop a timeline with crucial dates and events. You get the idea: just ensure that the notes you make are well structured, topic-by-topic, and that they draw out accurate and relevant information.

KNOW BOTH SIDES OF THE ARGUMENT, BUT CHOOSE WHICH SIDE YOU'LL BE IN FAVOUR OF

Depending on what subject you are revising for, it may also be important to condense key arguments and analysis for both sides of a discussion. In general (although your exam may be different), if you have to discuss or argue in favour of one argument over one or many others, the best technique is to learn information for all sides of the debate. However, it is also crucial that you decide which side you are going to be most in favour of.

> **Tip**
> Remember that the examiner does not care what your personal opinion is. I would always recommend arguing in favour of the side for which you have most points, ensuring that you play to your strengths in the exam, rather than focusing on your true beliefs.

You may find it useful to create a table with an argument on one side, and the counter-argument on the other. This way, you'll easily be able to see which side seems to be the stronger of the two.

Making sure you have these ideas on both sides of arguments condensed and learnt is just as important as learning the hard facts required to write a well-informed essay. There is no point in knowing a quotation from a philosopher if you don't know the arguments on both sides of the issue being discussed by the philosopher in that quotation. Equally, you must know where you'll choose to stand on arguments central to your course before the exam itself as many of the issues you may have to discuss will be extremely controversial and you risk wasting valuable time just trying to work out which side of your argument will be strongest.

START EARLY

Try and start making your these notes as early as possible, as they'll come in very useful when it comes to making essay-plans, and writing model essays (you'll learn about this shortly). Not only will condensing your course down help you revise all of the material, but it will also help you prioritise the most important information.

FIND YOUR SYLLABUS & MARK SCHEME

If you are struggling to know exactly what it is you need to put into your revision notes, look up the subject syllabus specific to your exam board. This is very useful, as it will bullet point exactly what it is you need to be revising. Look at both the subject content (what is included in your course syllabus), and assessment objectives (these are what the examiners expect of students during the exams themselves) to make sure that you know exactly what is expected of you. Again, it is important to do this early on in your revision so that you ensure you know exactly what you need to be revising

> **Tip**
> You will be able to find most of these syllabuses online, but if you're struggling, ask your teacher, as they will have access to them.

PAST PAPERS & MODEL ESSAY PLANS

Whilst it is never wise to try and predict exam questions, looking for regular themes and wordings of the questions is an invaluable part of your preparation. Exams are set by a variety of boards, and they all have differing layouts and expectations of students. By reading through past papers you can familiarise yourself with exactly what your specific exam board expects you to do in the exam.

Model essay plans are a great way of preparing for the types of question you might be faced with in a particular exam. Whilst studying and condensing the content of your course, you also need to get to grips with the arguments and structures of the sorts of essays you'll have to write in the exam.

TRY PLANNING PAST PAPER QUESTIONS

Having read through a few past papers, try imagining how you would answer the questions. Make a short plan, and be sure to include a basic introduction and conclusion. What would your main argument have been? What would you have found challenging to write about? Does this highlight some gaps in your knowledge that you need to address? By doing this, not only do you solidify the content (facts and arguments) in your mind, but you are also forced to think about the ways in which key arguments from particular topics can be used in conjunction with one another to form an essay.

PLAN THEMATICALLY

It is also important to plan some essays based around themes that are regularly tested by your exam board, and that are likely to come up on the day of your exam. For example, if your history syllabus details that students should know "how Stalin controlled the Soviet Union", produce a plan that enables you to hit the key points detailed in your condensed notes on this topic, structuring these in a logical way that separates out each method used by Stalin.

KNOW WHAT IS EXPECTED OF YOU

It is absolutely crucial here to know what the examiner would be expecting of you. If the question/syllabus/mark scheme states that you only need to provide a description, don't stray into debate. However, if you are informed that you need to structure an argument, make sure your essay revolves around one!

ACCUSTOM YOURSELF TO PLANNING FOR DIFFERENT TYPES OF QUESTION LIKELY TO APPEAR IN YOUR EXAM

Most examiners will set a very similar style of exam year after year, with different types of questions worth different numbers of marks that require you to respond in different ways. As such, you would be foolish not to accustom yourself to writing out plans for each of the different types of question that the examiner is likely to ask you, based on the structure of questions asked in past papers.

Is there a short, information-based question worth a few marks, followed by a longer descriptive question, followed by a long argumentative essay? Work out exactly what sort of questions your exam board is likely to ask you and make sure you know how each of these types of question should be answered. Then, plan how you would answer each of these types of question, ensuring you give everything the examiner is looking for.

> **Tip**
> Examiners' reports for past papers and examiners' sample papers and answers are great places to find exactly what the examiners themselves are looking for in the answers to their questions. All of this should be available online from your exam board's website.

So, for the example above, is your exam likely to ask you to simply detail each of the methods used by Stalin in order to control the

Soviet Union, or will you probably have to evaluate the strengths and weaknesses of each method, before coming to a conclusion as to which method was most effective? Perhaps you could be asked either of these. In any case, you should plan each possibility, at least in your head, considering exactly how you might use each of the pieces of information you've learnt.

Essays come in all shapes and sizes, and being able to structure your essay in the way the examiner intended guarantees you'll obtain a higher mark than if you come up with a structure on the day of the exam with no prior experience of how your essay should be written.

BEWARE OF THE DANGER OF PLANNING ESSAYS

Despite all of the benefits of essay planning as part of your revision, it does come with an inherent risk.

> *It's tempting, if you've crafted several essay plans, to try and use them, even if they don't quite fit the question being asked.*

The danger in this is that the examiner will think that you've misunderstood or misread the question, or even more perilously, will think you've simply pre-learnt an essay to write out, whatever the title. An essay plan can be flawless, but if it fails to correctly answer the question, you won't be given the marks you deserve.

With this in mind, it is essential that you practice moulding your plan to accommodate for variations of a question. For example, if you've planned for the question: *Is gothic writing a disturbing exploration of the unknown?* how might you answer the question: *Is gothic writing exciting because it explores the unknown?* Whilst the questions seem very similar, they are asking very different things, with one asking you to discuss exactly what gothic writing *is,* and the other asking you to argue about what makes gothic writing exciting.

That said, preparing essay plans should definitely form part of your revision... Just be careful when using them in exams!

ESSAY TECHNIQUE

WRITING TIMED ESSAYS

Essay planning is a fantastic way of getting to grips with arguments and information, but is much less useful when it comes to practicing your essay technique.

> *An essay question tests both a student's knowledge and writing ability. As a result, it is critical that you practice the skill of writing itself.*

Writing an essay under timed conditions is quite different to doing a practice paper in many other subjects (science, maths etc.) for a variety of reasons. Firstly, writing timed essays should come at the end of your revision of a certain topic. This is because unless you know the content and basic structures you want to employ, you simply won't be able to write for an extended period of time.

Whilst you can have a go at several questions from a maths paper that are relevant to that day's revision, sitting down to write a long essay actually requires a great deal of preparation. I would suggest that you do an essay question specific to the topic you are revising, when you feel you've already revised it rigorously. Regard it as a test to show how well you've understood the topic in question. Make sure you do it under timed conditions, hand written (unless you are permitted to use a laptop in your exam), and without any assistance from any notes.

It is also quite difficult, as a student, to mark an essay paper correctly. Unlike maths and the science, there is often not a specific mark scheme with right or wrong answers, and as a consequence marking your own paper might not be an option. Consequently, I would always suggest sending your practice essay questions to a teacher. If this is not possible, you can download the mark schemes to give yourself a rough idea of how you did, but this is not preferable.

> **Note**
> Again, this depends on the type of essay you're writing. If you are practicing a section that requires a simple description, the mark scheme should be enough to tell you how many marks you would have scored.

PRACTICE PARAGRAPHS

Writing timed essays is invaluable but is, by its nature, very time consuming. As a result of this, I would suggest practicing your technique on a smaller scale as well as on a larger scale.

Writing single paragraphs, or extracts of an essay can be incredibly useful, preparing you to deploy the content and arguments you've learnt in a concise manner. Rather than writing the whole essay, simply write an extract on areas that you feel you might struggle talking about. For example, write a paragraph arguing that thwarted love is the main theme of *The Great Gatsby*, or that the assassination of Franz Ferdinand wasn't in fact the driving force behind the start of World War I.

Learning how to argue convincingly (or describe depending on what is expected of you by the exam board), and most importantly hitting the key points in the mark scheme in a paragraph is essential for exam success. Make sure you hit all the assessment objectives or bullet points in the mark scheme, and practice doing this in every paragraph you write.

ESSAY-BASED SUBJECTS
PART II: EXAM TECHNIQUE
(BY CAMERON ANDERSON)

CHOOSE QUESTIONS WISELY

Quite simply make sure you take the time at the start of the exam to choose which questions you are going to answer. If you have to choose questions from different sections, be certain to do as your told and answer the right number of questions from each section. Then, think about the exact questions: you may have a great essay plan for the causes of World War I, but if the question asks about the results, you won't be answering the question. Having said this, don't waste too much time on this; have a look, assess the situation and make a decision.

RTFQ – ATFQ

… Read the flipping question – Answer the flipping question. It is likely that you've heard this phrase before, but it crucial that you understand its importance. Misunderstanding a single question in an essay-based paper can be the difference between an A* and a C. Therefore, it is essential that you are diligent when reading the question. Make sure you are aware of exactly what is being asked of you. Does the question ask you to evaluate, compare, describe, debate, or discuss the topic at hand? Read the question, and read it again. Reading through past papers and mark schemes will hopefully have given you some idea what kind of question the examiner will be asking, but making sure you check, and check again is crucial.

Answering the question is also of paramount importance.

> *After you've read and understood what is being asked of you, you must make sure that your answer is tailored towards what the examiner wants to see.*

Whilst this advice might seem obvious, it is tempting, if you've planned a slightly different essay in your revision, or dislike the topic the question is steering you towards, to ignore it and only half answer the question. This is a big mistake. The examiner will pick up that you haven't fully answered what is being asked of you, and you'll receive a lower mark. Even if the wording of a question makes it more difficult to answer, actually answering it will still result in higher marks.

PLANNING

Ensure you always start by spending 5 minutes planning the essay at hand, rather than diving straight in and then realising that you've missed out details you

Tip
For comparative essays, make sure you've planned out the key points of comparison, and in which paragraphs you want to hit these points. For descriptive essays, plan out the descriptions paragraph-by-paragraph.

wanted to include or that you've totally messed up your essay's structure. Beginning an essay without a plan is never a good idea, even if you feel confident that you know what you're going to write. Make sure you have a rough idea of what you want to say in your introduction as well as an overarching plan of your essay's structure, detailing the direction in which you want it to progress.

Make sure you know roughly how you want to conclude, and list any key quotes or details that are essential, so you don't forget to include them. Make sure you include paragraphs, and have an idea in your plan of what you want each paragraph to contain.

Having some structure to your essay is essential, and having practiced making essay plans during your revision, you should be able to produce one swiftly. However, don't feel obliged to follow your plan entirely if you feel you want to go down another route halfway through your essay. Sometimes you might realise that your plan failed to account for an important point, or that you feel another argument is stronger. Sticking religiously to your plan is unnecessary, and can sometimes result in less exciting essays. However, planning is still essential for developing a good structure and pace within your essay.

STRONG ARGUMENTS & WEAK ARGUMENTS – AVOIDING THE FENCE

This section only really applies to students who are writing essays that require arguing two or more sides of a debate. However, a lot of essay-based exams have at least one question that involves something of this sort, so it is a good idea to know how to approach this style of question.

It is tempting, with these sorts of questions, to argue for one side and then for the other, concluding in mutual agreement with both sides. Essentially, it is tempting to 'sit on the fence'. My advice is to be a little more adventurous. Really think about which side of your argument appears stronger from your plan and then go with it! Make sure that you establish the other side of the argument, why people support it, and why it might be convincing, but do not suggest that it is the "correct" opinion. Exciting essays are weighted towards one side of the argument, and explain *why* it is the better side of the argument. Examiners will read hundreds of "on the one hand, one the other" scripts, but very few that argue convincingly for one side.

Sometimes, you might find yourself in mutual agreement with the arguments. This is okay! If this is the case then you'll have genuine cause to "sit on the fence," and your essay should be convincing regardless. However, if your argument is agreeing with one side more than the other, make sure you let the examiner know this.

> **Tip**
> Remember that it is crucial that you answer the questions in the way the examiner intends. As such, you should look at the mark schemes and examiner reports to find out whether your exam board wants you to 'sit on the fence' or not with this style of question.

TIMING

Keeping an eye on the time is crucial during essay-based exams, as you'll usually have to divide your time between questions. For example, if you have to write four essays in three hours, then it is wise to give yourself 43 minutes an essay, leaving 8 minutes at the end to check over your spelling and grammar. If the essays are worth varying numbers of marks, then divide your time proportionately. Typically, the more marks an essay is worth, the longer it needs to be.

You are more likely to run out of time in essay-based exams than in any other, and so you must make sure you are rigorous with your timing.

> *Try not to write for an extra five minutes on one essay, only to sacrifice time on another.*

If you are really pushed for time, it is better to cut into the time you should have left for spell checking at the end.

In a worst-case scenario where you run out of time, bullet point the final parts of the essay you are working on. Always include a conclusion, even if it is in a bullet point format. This will show the examiner where you were going with your essay, and is likely to gain you at least a few extra marks. Obviously writing a full essay is preferable, and this should always be your aim. The bullet point method is your last resort.

Conclusions

It is fitting that we should finish this chapter with some advice on conclusions. A good conclusion will summarise your essay, condensing your argument into a few hard hitting lines that perfectly convey what you've been writing about.

If you are concluding a descriptive piece, make sure you give an overview of what you've been discussing through the exam question at hand. Conclusions are a way of telling the examiner you've finished, and that you've understood and answered the question. Make sure your argument is obvious, and make sure you state why it is the correct answer to the question.

However, for those students who wish to dazzle the examiner, I would advise adding something *new* in your conclusion. A good conclusion will summarise and condense an argument, but an excellent conclusion will bring something original to the table. It doesn't have to be much, perhaps a simple rhetorical question, or the beginnings of a new argument. Maybe point out a flaw in the question, or specify where it was unclear or ambiguous. This can be very difficult to do, especially when one is pushed for time, and it is by no means essential. But if you have the time, and the capacity, finishing with a little flair can go a long way.

MATHS & SCIENCE
PART I : REVISION (BY DAVID MORRIS)

MAKE YOUR OWN REVISION GUIDE

Learning is best accomplished by doing. Writing your own little guide not only helps you engrain information into your head, but also allows you to format and structure it as you please.

Your guide should contain information you struggled to understand or that you got wrong while doing questions from homework or past papers. It should also include any equations or definitions that you find difficult to commit to memory. Finally, ensure you leave plenty of space between different sections on different topics in your revision guide so that you can add things later as you do more and more past papers...

DO PAST PAPERS IN WAVES

More so than in most other subjects, this is a guaranteed way to increase your chances of success. It simply comes down to the fact that there are only so many types of question the examiners can ask, and only so many different ways they can test your knowledge of what is essentially the same information.

The best way of using past papers is to do them in waves. It is up to you whether you would like to start your revision with a past paper, or whether you would like to try and revise all of the material, focusing on what you find most difficult, first. Either way, the key is that you revise before attempting a/another past paper. When you've marked the past paper, focus your revision on any areas you found particularly difficult during your next revision sessions, and then do another past paper, and so on!

When you make mistakes in past papers, add these along with any helpful explanation to your personal revision guide in the spaces you have left available.

LOOK FOR PATTERNS

Maths and science are all about logic and patterns, so why not use it in your revision? If you've done a good few past papers you'll have noticed that there's always a question about circles, and there's always a question where you have to do algebra / probability etc. Use this knowledge to your advantage. Make a page of A4 listing all the types of questions that come up frequently. This small task can help you break down what the course is asking of you, and will almost certainly make your revision more efficient.

MAKE SURE YOU UNDERSTAND EVERYTHING

If you still don't understand something once you've revised it, make sure you ask your teacher. Understanding every single part of the course is key to ensuring you don't come unstuck on the day of the exam when the examiner throws in a question on the one section you don't fully understand.

LOOK THROUGH THE FORMULA BOOKLET

This is so utterly simple yet many people don't utilise the formula booklet to its full extent. Many science and maths exams are done with the help of a formula booklet. I'll talk more about this in exam technique, but in terms of revision, make sure you know what is available to help you in the formula booklet, where it is, and what it's used for. This should be done well in advance of your exam; your teacher should be able to show or lend you a copy of your exam board's formula booklet.

Often there'll be formulae or definitions hidden in your formula booklet so that they don't look quite like the one you've learnt. Don't let the examiners fool you: look through carefully as part of your revision.

Know your calculator

If you've bought a new scientific calculator for your maths or science course (and I strongly advise you do – my personal recommendation is the Casio FX-991ES with solar panels) then the chances are it can do some pretty neat things to help you. Some calculators can do pretty much anything you ask them and have features to help you with all kinds of calculations. Know how to use these features and become familiar so that you're quick.

However, do not just use the calculator, as this will get you no marks. You should get into the habit of writing out formulae and doing calculations the long way so that the examiner can see your method clearly. Then use these features to check your answers at the end.

MATHS & SCIENCE
PART II : EXAM TECHNIQUE
(BY DAVID MORRIS)

BE PREPARED IN ADVANCE

You've been told before: "Make sure you have all of your equipment (pencils, black inked pens, ruler and calculator) ready before the morning of the day of your exam." However, being prepared in advance is much more than just this. You should:

- Know and be familiar with how your calculator works, having practiced doing and checking different types of question using it.
- Have a good idea what the exam you are going to be taking looks like, but also be prepared for the unforeseen as there is no guarantee the examiner won't throw in something completely unexpected.
- Have worked out how many 'marks per minute' you need to complete in order to finish on time. If there are 120 marks available for a paper and the paper is 2 hours long, you have one mark per minute. Obviously some questions worth 1 or 2 marks will take you much less than a minute, so you'll have slightly longer on the explanation questions worth 3 marks or more. That said, you should also try to leave 10 minutes of checking time at the end.

KEEP YOUR ANSWERS TO THE POINT

Let's say there's a question you know the answer to, worth 4 marks. As much as you may suddenly think: "I know this one!" and then be tempted to start to splurge ideas in the answer space, you must resist! Take a moment to think what the 4 different points on the mark scheme will be and then, quite simply, write a single, precise sentence for each. This will gain you maximum marks in minimal time.

USE YOUR CALCULATOR

... Even when you think you know the answer. You may think you can do $13 \times 13 = 169$ in your head but in the heat of the moment, you shouldn't take anything for granted. Type it into your calculator; it'll only take a second. Make full use of the features available, which make calculations easier and allow you to check answers accurately and quickly.

USE THE FORMULA BOOKLET

In a similar way to using your calculator, even when you think you know the answer, you should use the formula booklet to make sure you've written down each formula correctly. In many cases an incorrect formula will get you zero marks as it shows a thorough lack of understanding, even if you've only made a small mistake.

CHECK YOUR ANSWERS

It's a given that if you have time at the end of an exam you should use it to check your answers, but how you do this will (and should) vary between different subjects.

DO IT AGAIN USING A DIFFERENT METHOD

In maths and science, there is a trick that I use regularly when possible to give me ultimate confidence in my answer: do the question or part of the question again using a completely different method.

Using your calculator to jump to the answer is an example of this, but often if you've revised hard you'll have realised that you can often do a question in two (or sometimes even more) different ways. If you're balancing forces and used equilibrium in your first attempt, why not use moments in your second? If you've found acceleration using the SUVAT equations, now try differentiating velocity.

Of course, your ability to answer questions in a variety of ways comes down to each student's individual course and stage of education, so if you didn't understand any of that, don't worry too much; the point is to try and check your answer by doing the question in a slightly different way.

<u>DO IT AGAIN</u>
If you cannot think of an alternative way to answer a question check it in the traditional sense: do it again as if you hadn't done it before.

'SHOW THAT...' QUESTIONS

It's relatively common in maths and science exams to get some questions beginning with the words 'show that'. If you've got no idea how to begin in order to reach the desired answer, try starting from the given answer (writing it at the bottom of your page) and try to write the line of working immediately before that one. Use logic and what you know about the course to help you. For example, (again, don't worry if you don't understand this) if the given answer involves a $\tan(\theta)$ term then try turning this into $\frac{\sin\theta}{\cos\theta}$ and see if this makes things any clearer.

LANGUAGES
PART I : REVISION
(BY LIAM PORRITT, ADAM BENNETT & ALEX VAN LEEUWEN)

LEARN VOCAB

You may like to learn vocab using websites or apps, in which case, we recommend trying as many as you possibly can so that you find the one that most suits your learning style. However, if, like us, you still prefer using a physical vocab list, or if you are given one to learn by your teacher, this section will help you discover the most efficient way of learning it.

There are obviously several methods to learning vocab, each of which will suit different people to different degrees. Some might like to record themselves saying the list, then listen to it repeatedly. Others may like to write it out themselves. You may find it helpful to group words into different sections – such as nouns, verbs, adjectives etc. – to offer an alternative order to the one provided in the original list. The key is finding a method that works for you.

We like to use the following 4-step process:

STEP 1
Go through the list before you start learning it. There'll probably be lots you don't know, but this step is to mark off the ones you do. There's no point in constantly reviewing words you've known for years. Mark them off, and move on.

STEP 2
Go through the list, systematically trying to learn the words. You may also find it helpful to come up with ways of

remembering words you find difficult to commit to memory (have a look at pg. 102 for more).

The key is to do this little and often: learn it in small chunks, but regularly.

STEP 3
After you feel confident that you've learned a section, test yourself on it. At that point, mark the ones you've got wrong. You should be sure to test yourself in a different order each time so that you ensure you are not merely learning the order of the words.

STEP 4
Write these words you got wrong on a separate sheet of paper – this way, you're again only testing yourself on the ones you don't know. You may also find that the process of writing out the more difficult words helps you to learn them.

KNOW YOUR GRAMMAR

In language exams, the chances are that you'll be either tested specifically on your grammatical knowledge or expected to display that you can use the language accurately, without making grammatical errors.

Grammar is something that lots of people seem to find scary and, frankly, boring. However, when learning languages, there are some fairly fundamental rules that simply need to be learnt in order for you to stand a chance of success. So, again, it really is just a case of reassuring yourself that it'll be worth it when you come away with outstanding grades at the end of it all. Plus, being able to whip out a well-constructed sentence in a foreign language is sure to impress any potential employers... or any young ladies/gents for that matter!

BREAK IT DOWN

Having a sound grasp of the grammar of a language is a vital part of exam success. Grammar is, however, so extensive and often complicated that it is difficult to know where to start. To combat this it is important that you break down grammar revision into different grammar points, such as pronouns or regular verbs of a certain conjugation. From here you can identify which grammar points you are less comfortable with and which you feel you know well.

The key is to not let yourself get disheartened. Grammar in any language is hugely complicated. Indeed, even a native speaker would find certain questions regarding the grammar of their language difficult. Start with what you know you struggle with and attack it head on; grammar learning always takes time but often, with perseverance, you reach a eureka moment and achieve a solid understanding of what you previously found confusing.

LEARN PATTERNS

Once you've broken down grammar into different parts, the key is to remember

> **Tip**
> Try saying patterns, such as verb endings, out loud to help them stick in your mind.

patterns that can be applied to each of these sets of words. You should look for similarities and differences between distinct grammatical groups (such as those between 'er' and 're' verbs in French), as this will help you memorise their patterns.

FOCUS ON THE BASICS

While there are often many irregularities in languages, we would strongly advise that you focus on the regular patterns first.

> *If you make mistakes on irregulars (particularly obscure ones), it is forgivable. However, basic errors are likely to cost you dearly.*

For example, regular verb conjugations must be learnt well, along with any common irregulars, such as the verb 'to be' (irregular in nearly all languages).

Furthermore, by tying together all that you've been learning and applying it to proper sentences, you'll find that your understanding and grasp of those individual topics will be greatly improved.

LEARN PHRASES AND STRUCTURES

Learning phrases and, more importantly, learning to manipulate and use them in different circumstances is absolutely essential if you want to obtain the best grade possible. For your writing and oral examinations, these phrases will allow you to really take the standard of your essay or answer to the next level.

The easiest way to learn them is to come up with a list of your favourite phrases that show off your grammatical knowledge – if you want to find some, there are loads in Liam's Exam Grade Booster GCSE language guides, which can be applied to pretty much any language exam, even if it isn't a GCSE – and then to begin to include these in different practice essays and answers. Get used to their structure and to using them in different ways, such as with different people (not just 'I', but also with 'he', 'we' or 'they'), and with different topics. The key is not only to have pre-learnt structures, but also to be able to manipulate them.

UNDERSTAND WHAT IS REQUIRED OF YOU

This applies to all subjects, but is particularly crucial in language exams. You must have a good look at past papers and mark schemes to ensure that you know exactly what examiners are looking for. Is the quality of your language as important as the content? Should you spend more time being very careful when writing your essay, or are you required to write lots under time pressure? Work out the answers to these sorts of questions before the big day.

APPLY WHAT YOU KNOW

Even more so than with any other subject, you must practice manipulating your knowledge so that you can give the examiners exactly what they are looking for.

Rounding up everything you've been revising and applying it to full sentences and paragraphs is a key part of language exam preparation. It is great to be able to conjugate every different verb in a given tense or to understand the role of the indefinite article; however, all of this is wasted if you cannot apply this knowledge in the exam.

When revising for languages, therefore, it is crucial that you practice writing and using that foundational work you've been doing. You should do grammar exercises to ensure you're able to apply your grammatical knowledge. However, writing or saying full sentences, either to questions or in an essay is undeniably the best way to apply what you know. Practice is key.

> *The more I practice, the luckier I get.*
>
> Gary Player (Golfer)

LANGUAGES
PART II : EXAM TECHNIQUE
(BY LIAM PORRITT & ADAM BENNETT)

WRITE WHAT YOU KNOW, DON'T WRITE WHAT YOU DON'T KNOW

So often in language exams we come up with a great idea for a sentence or an answer in English and then try to translate it into the relevant language. This approach does not work!

Ultimately, our grasp of English is obviously more advanced than that of the languages we are being examined on. Furthermore, very often things we say in English are said very differently in other languages so attempting to transliterate in this way can lead to virtually incomprehensible sentences. For example, 'it's raining cats and dogs' is unlikely to be expressed in the same way in the foreign language.

Instead, you should think what you know (vocab, grammar and phrases) and fit that into your essay.

QUALITY OVER COMPLEXITY

It is vital to remember that, very often in language exams, the majority of marks are given to the quality and accuracy of your language rather than the complexity of your ideas. As a result, your emphasis should lie on producing accurate sentences and answers and not on creating intellectually complicated ideas. This is where the technique of pre-prepared phrases will come into its own, allowing you to produce linguistically impressive pieces of writing rather than struggling to think of complex sentences on the spot.

DON'T PANIC OVER ONE WORD!

When tackling a reading or listening exam it is easy to panic when we miss or don't understand a word. Remember that your success in an exam will not hinge on one single word!

Of course it is annoying when we feel that some of the words we don't understand are important to answering a question, however, often we can work out the sense of the word from context or even answer the question without knowing what a few words mean.

By getting frustrated or worried over minor gaps in vocabulary we waste time, throw our focus and, when it comes to listening exams, risk missing subsequent information.

CONCLUSION

Now Go and Succeed

So, there we have it. Follow all of those rules and you'll be a long way towards achieving exam success.

The most important thing to remember is that hard work does pay off. I truly believe that anyone is able to achieve anything (within reason) if they are willing to dedicate enough high-quality time to improving their own ability.

Remember to study smart as well as hard... And if you can, try to enjoy what you are studying. Bear in mind that you are receiving an education that people all over the world are literally dying to obtain, so make the most of it.

Let me know your thoughts

If you've found this guide helpful or think it could be improved, I would be hugely grateful if you could let me know what you think of it by sending me an email to liam@examgradebooster.com.

If you've liked it, please do also leave a review on Amazon so that other people are encouraged to discover *The Rules of Revision*.

Congratulations

All that is left for me to say is a massive well done for getting this far. Now you need to go and commit to putting these rules into practice so that you obtain the grades you deserve.

The Rules

Plan to Succeed
Rule 1: Learn it in the First Place
Rule 2: Sort out your Filing System
Rule 3: Plan Yourself
Rule 4: Plan Realistically
Rule 5: Plan Precisely
Rule 6: Give Yourself Small Goals & Rewards
Rule 7: Don't Lose Sight of the Bigger Picture
Rule 8: Be Flexible & Have Contingency Slots
Rule 9: Revise Early
Rule 10: Plan Different Types of Revision
Rule 11: Take Breaks… But, How Often? How Long?
Rule 12: Prioritise
Rule 13: Don't Have Lots of Days Off
Rule 14: Revise your Revision

Study Smarter
Rule 15: Believe You Can Revise Effectively
Rule 16: Remember: Everyone is in the Same Boat
Rule 17: Stick to the Plan
Rule 18: Find a Healthy Study Environment
Rule 19: Choose Music Wisely
Rule 20: Make your Body your Temple
Rule 21: Sleep
Rule 22: Know How You Revise
Rule 23: Condense Everything
Rule 24: Test Yourself
Rule 25: Understand what you Revise
Rule 26: Make Facts Relatable
Rule 27: Find Ways to Remember what to Remember
Rule 28: Avoid Distractions
Rule 29: During Breaks, Get Out
Rule 30: Make Technology your Friend
Rule 31: Teach & Learn Outside the Classroom
Rule 32: Do Past Papers Properly

RULE 33: DON'T FEAR BEING WRONG
RULE 34: ACTUALLY REVISE

OPTIMISE EXAM PERFORMANCE
RULE 35: NO ALL-NIGHTERS
RULE 36: DON'T BURN OUT
RULE 37: PMA
RULE 38: CONTROL STRESS... AND THEN EMBRACE IT
RULE 39: GET EVERYTHING SORTED IN ADVANCE
RULE 40: AVOID CHOKING
RULE 41: EARN MARKS SHREWDLY
RULE 42: ANSWER THE QUESTION

FOLLOW US ONLINE

Discover loads of useful resources and find out about all of our current and future products by joining the Exam Grade Booster community online.

VISIT US:
WWW.EXAMGRADEBOOSTER.COM

CHECK OUT OUR BLOG:
WWW.BLOG.EXAMGRADEBOOSTER.COM

FOLLOW US:
@EXAMGRADEBOOSTER

LIKE US:
EXAM GRADE BOOSTER

FOLLOW US:
@EXAMGRADEBOOST

WRITE FOR US

WANT TO BECOME AN AUTHOR YOURSELF?

WANT TO EARN MONEY?

WANT TO HAVE SOMETHING HUGELY IMPRESSIVE ON YOUR CV?

Yes, yes, yes!

Go to www.examgradebooster.com and find the *Write for Us* page. This page should have all the information you are after, but if you have any other questions you can contact us via the website.

In order to write for us, you'll have to complete a very straight-forward application process (there is a short form to fill out at the bottom of the *Write for Us* page).

Should you be deemed suitable to write a book, you'll be given access to all of our manuscripts, formatting, cover design and branding as well as having the immediate advantage of working with people, just like yourself, who have succeeded in writing their very own books.

Exam Grade Booster

Made in the USA
Coppell, TX
10 March 2023

14088480R00114